ZIMBABWE

Journey through
ZIMBABWE

Mohamed Amin · Duncan Willetts
Brian Tetley

MPC

Acknowledgements

We would like to thank the many organizations and people throughout Zimbabwe who gave us help and advice in the production of this book, in particular Air Zimbabwe, Ian Cochrane of Zimbabwe Sun Hotels, Brian Bowyer and Phibean Chawatama of the United Touring Company and Peter Dunjey of the Bulawayo Publicity Association. We are also indebted to Ed Moyo, John Edlin and Angus Shaw for their help in verifying facts and information.

First published 1990 by
Moorland Publishing Co. Ltd.,
Moor Farm Road,
Ashbourne,
Derbyshire DE6 1HD
England

© Camerapix 1990

ISBN 0 86190 341 2

British Library Cataloguing in Publication Data:
Amin, Mohamed
    Journey through Zimbabwe
    1. Zimbabwe — Description and travel
    I. Title II. Willetts, Duncan
    III. Tetley, Brian

This book was designed and produced by
Camerapix Publishers International,
P.O. Box 45048,
Nairobi, Kenya

Edited by John Barraclough
Design: Craig Dodd
Production Editor: Debbie Gaiger
Typeset: Kimberly Davis

From half-title to contents pages: Tonga woman; Zambezi darter; tobacco plantation; national flag carrier; sunny Zimbabweans; elephant and young; trotting at Harare; white rhino; and leopard.

Endpapers: Ancient bushman rock paintings at Silozwane, Matobo Hills.

Contents

1. Introduction:
Journey through Zimbabwe

Sundown over the Zambezi Valley, a flaming flare path of molten fire laid on the still waters of Lake Kariba through the lengthening shadows of a 'drowned forest', is the lasting image of Zimbabwe that most visitors remember. The image is refreshingly new in an ancient land. Half a century ago Lake Kariba did not exist.

Nature — and man — constantly reshape the glory that is Zimbabwe. Born many millions of centuries ago it wears its age as graciously as a bearded sage. But it is also as young as tomorrow and celebrates its youth in the tingling sparkle of its many new wonders, of which perhaps the Kariba sunset is the most magnificent.

Yet without a great body of water no land can claim true beauty. And there was none in this land — neither in its tawny deserts filled with elephant and lion, nor among its savannah plains, where antelope, buffalo, rhino, and myriad creatures roamed.

Nor any in its sweltering, humid lowlands and none on the fertile highveld soils that covered the staggering mineral riches buried deep beneath.

Among its craggy peaks and hidden valleys were only thundering, cascading falls and bright, capricious streams singing at their sudden, joyous release from the thickly-forested escarpments and open, rolling moorlands.

Water there was in abundance but no lake or sea. Indeed, there was water in such plenitude that where, over the millenniums, the currents of the mighty Zambezi probed the rock faults and fissures of its ancient bed it carved not one but eight successive precipices (and has now begun to carve a ninth) to form one of the greatest physical spectacles in Africa — a wall of constantly falling water almost two kilometres wide that plunges vertically more than 300 feet into a narrow gorge. This is 'Mosi-oa-Tunya', 'the smoke that thunders', known around the world as the Victoria Falls.

Thus, high and landlocked, Zimbabwe needed only one thing to complete its beauty as a land of contrasts, one thing in which all life rejoices — an ocean or an inland sea.

Many millions of years ago there was such a sea, so large that none of its shores could be seen from the other. But that sea had been sucked dry by the remorseless African sun long before the first Bantu migrations at least a thousand years or more ago into the land of the 'San', the original Bushmen inhabitants.

So, early this century, man began to lay his hand upon the land. Streams were blocked and rivers dammed all across the country that was to become Zimbabwe.

Then, during the 1950s, upstream from a deep gorge, half a kilometre wide, in the north-east corner of the Zambezi Valley, many hundreds toiled and eighty-seven died to build the Kariba dam. Now, where once there was only a narrow river gorge, the cool waters of a new great African lake spread out over more than 5,000 square kilometres of once parched earth.

Long and slender, stretching almost 300 kilometres from south-west to north-east and more than forty kilometres across its widest north-south axis, Lake Kariba was the final brush stroke that transformed Zimbabwe into a land of ineradicable beauty.

Opposite: In spate the Victoria Falls forms the largest curtain of falling water in the world.

If nature and man combined to transform the landscape, it is man alone who has endowed Zimbabwe with its enduring legacy of art and cultures — rock paintings and engravings etched during the last 20,000 years on the walls of granite cliffs and caves; cities and fortresses that beginning around 2,000 years ago were built systematically to ordered design and achieved their fulfilment in the ancient civilization of Great Zimbabwe which blossomed between the eleventh and thirteenth centuries; and in a treasury of stone sculpture that belongs solely to the twentieth century.

Man who built the clean and spacious towns and cities that, with their immensely wide streets, shaded by jacaranda and flamboyants and lined by bougainvillaea and sweet-scented shrubs and flowers, seem to belong exclusively to the twenty-first century.

Man who ploughed and watered the highveld and the middleveld to see them burgeon with prairies of wheat and maize, plantations of sugarcane and tobacco, meadows of fruit and flowers; man who stocked the more arid ranges with beef and dairy cattle and made the highland slopes verdant with emerald-green tea bushes, olive-coloured coffee trees, and fruitful vineyards.

And only man who tapped its rivers for power to fuel his industries and wrest from this remarkable country the mineral treasures of gold and silver, platinum and tungsten, copper and chrome, iron and steel, coal and limestone, lead and tin, magnesite and asbestos, emeralds and diamonds needed to develop his economy.

Yet never were nature and man more in harmony. All across Zimbabwe, interspersed between man's sturdy and sometimes scouring handiwork, are pristine and protected wildlife wildernesses, botanical and bird reserves, forest sanctuaries and many lakes that serve as fisheries and leisure playgrounds for anglers and watersports enthusiasts.

And it's not just simply harmony: here the seasons of the north are reversed and spring comes in September and October (though some call it autumn, for no apparent reason other than perhaps the fall colours that drape the trees).

Here, in the heart of Africa, where the new nation of Zimbabwe clings to the fabric of a turbulent, romantic, and fabled history stretching back thousands of years, and cultures and landscapes meld into a timeless mosaic that is both ancient and modern, is interwoven the more recent tragedy of European conquest. But what a triumphant outcome.

Initially, during the Stone Age, the San, small groups of hunter-gatherers, wandered thinly over the country's massive central plateau. Much later, these Khoisan-speaking communities were edged aside by waves of migrant Bantu agriculturists and pastoralists.

Long before Christ, man had started to domesticate the beasts and till the fields of what is now Zimbabwe. All across this sun-kissed land roamed herds of elephant and buffalo, prides of lion, families of leopard and cheetah, antelope and reclusive rhino.

Amid them, as ancient ruins testify, cultures and civilizations rose and flourished at a time when all the rest of the world thought of Africa only as dark, mysterious — and unknown.

The most powerful of these dynastic kingdoms, ancestors of today's

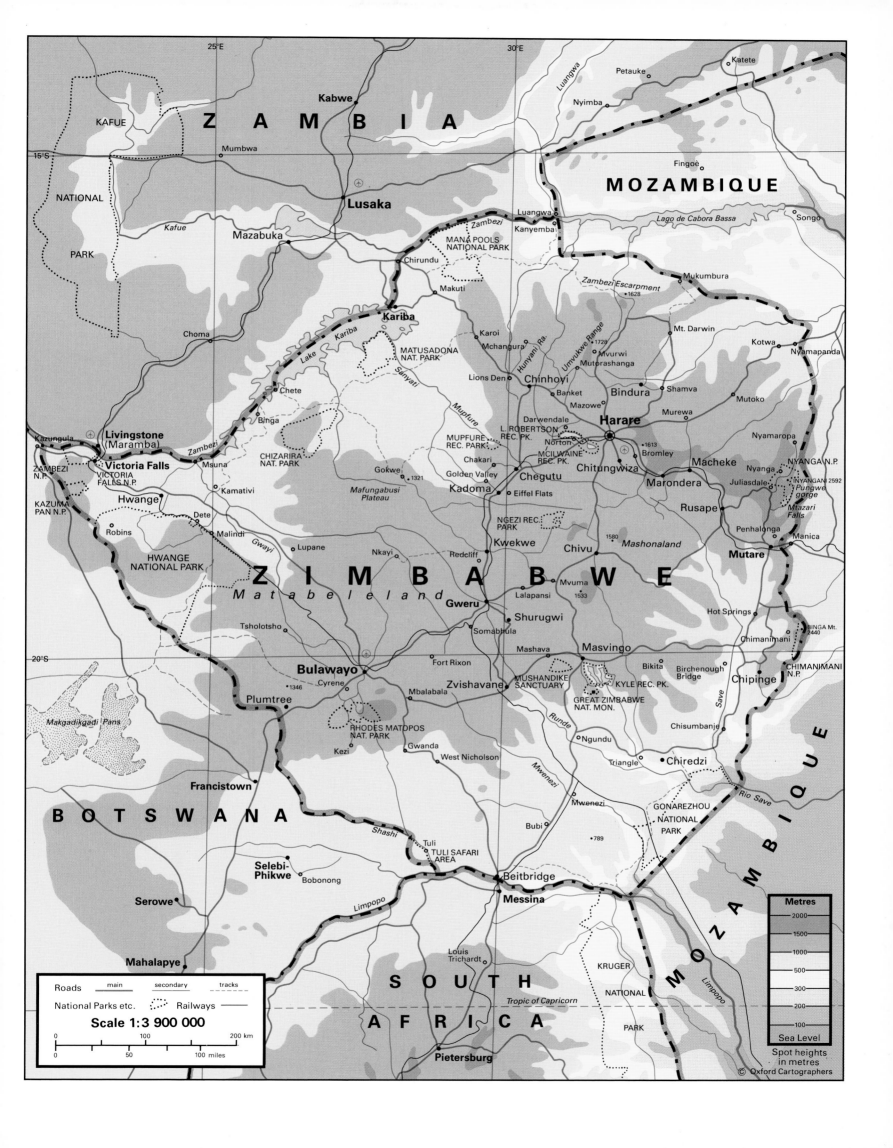

majority Shona communities, occupied much of southern and central Africa, as far west as Tati in what is now Botswana, to the coast of Mozambique in the east, and from the Limpopo to western Mozambique.

Early last century, these dynasties came into confrontation with the Zulu ancestors of today's Ndebele communities. The *impi*, warriors, of the Nguni who rebelled against the great warrior leader, Shaka Zulu, marched northwards and finally invaded the land of the Shona around 1820.

The last of these Zulu groups, the Khumalo, completed their conquests in the 1840s, establishing themselves in the south-west of modern Zimbabwe where King Mzilikazi built a new capital, Mhlahlandlela. Gradually they absorbed the people and cultures who had long lived there into their own and became the Ndebele.

Thus did the first Europeans who stepped this way just a few years later find this land of overwhelming beauty, with its proud and fierce tribes ready to die in its defence.

This rich, mysterious history inspired romantic fiction by such authors as Rider Haggard, who wrote *King Solomon's Mines*, that this

Above: Hwange National Park with white rhino and young in foreground; giraffe in background. The white rhino's name derives from the Afrikaans word 'weit' meaning square-lipped — not from its colour.

Above: Nile crocodiles have been translocated into many of Hwange's sixty artificial water pans to maintain natural predation in the ecosystem. A survivor from the age of the dinosaurs more than 160 million years ago, the country's rivers and lakes are being restocked by commercial crocodile farmers.

was the fabulous land of Ophir with the great treasure troves that sustained Solomon and Sheba — legends brought to life in the 1980s through a range of movies filmed on location in Zimabwbe.

Among the first European visitors was Dr. David Livingstone, the Christian missionary whose name is irrevocably linked with that of Zimbabwe. The prosaic but sensitive Scotsman was so overwhelmed by his first sight of the great falls on the Zambezi in 1855 that he momentarily abandoned his pragmatic scientific observations to wax — not without justification — rhapsodic.

'It had never been seen before by European eyes,' he wrote as he stood on an island at the edge of the cataract where the spray from the falls soaked him and his notebook, 'but scenes so lovely must have been gazed upon by angels in their flight.'

Loyally, the good missionary, whose heart lies buried in the continent to which he gave his life, named this great wonder of the world after Victoria, his British queen.

Livingstone's was a compassionate mission. But that of the other European whose name is also irrevocably linked with Zimbabwe — whose name indeed preceded it — was driven by both financial lust

Below: Tonga mother carries home the firewood.

Bottom: Young girl carries home banana leaves in the Honde Valley.

and visions of imperial grandeur.

In fulfilling the first, Cecil John Rhodes achieved the second and earned brief immortality as the 'father of the British Empire'.

It was all too brief for a man whose achievements in his short time were approximate to those of an epoch. But just over a century after Rhodes landed in South Africa, and eighty-three years after the lands of the Ndebele and Shona were named Rhodesia by British royal decree, Zimbabwe was born and Rhodes's statue was removed from the streets of the capital he named Salisbury, now Harare.

There were others with him of lesser stature whose names still prevail in the country's geography — for instance Beitbridge, the town named after his confidante and adviser, Alfred Beit.

Some Europeans who followed Livingstone but preceded Rhodes made their homes among the friendly Ndebele in their Matabeleland capital, then under Mzilikazi's successor, Lobengula. Others, like the hunter Frederick Courtney Selous, were more transitory, roaming the great wildernesses of Matabeleland and Mashonaland, seeking ivory, rhino horn and other trophies.

Still others came hurrying to trade with these African kingdoms or to live in the bush and pan the rivers and mine the rock for gold, silver, and gemstones.

From the moment Rhodes arrived at the Cape, on the southern tip of the continent, he set his heart on colonizing the length of Africa, from the Cape to Cairo, under the British flag. The first stage in his grand strategy was the annexation of the Zambezi basin and the Great African Lakes to the north.

To set about achieving this, he established the British South Africa Company — BSAC — under a royal charter signed by Victoria on 29 October, 1889.

Subsequently, Rhodes despatched mercenaries to Mashonaland where they built four fortresses — one named Fort Salisbury, after the incumbent British Prime Minister, Lord Salisbury. Here the company flag, incorporating the Union flag of Great Britain, was raised on 12 September, 1890.

Later, emissaries were sent to Bulawayo where — by ruses and deceits — Lobengula was duped into signing away Matabeleland. Though later this great leader perceived the deceit and repudiated the agreement, both Matabeleland and Mashonaland in effect had come under the British crown. The British South Africa Company's newly-acquired Maxim guns, mowing down all those who resisted, sealed the fact almost before the ink on the contract was dry.

Lobengula himself retreated north towards the Zambezi and died on the march in January 1894. In the aftermath, Rhodes took three of the ruler's sons into virtual slavery at his home on the Cape.

He now set about consolidating the power of the BSAC and, therefore, the Crown by expropriating all the arable and grazing land which Rhodes and his company claimed as their own property. Indeed, a great many Zimbabweans today still live on the arid Tribal Trust Lands defined in 1894 by the Land Commission that Rhodes established.

Perhaps the greatest irony is that Rhodes, who died in March 1902

Below: Harare schoolboy — the British influence still prevails in customs and dress.

Above: Young Ndebele child in the communal lands around Matobo National Park.

aged forty-eight, chose for his grave the natural grandeur of the Matobo Hills where Mzilikazi, the father of Lobengula, also lies buried.

As early as 1896, the Ndebele took up arms against colonial domination and although there were periods of acquiescence, the struggle for freedom never ceased. For ten brief years the two Rhodesias — southern and northern — and Nyasaland (now Malawi) formed a political and economic federation which ended when Northern Rhodesia attained Independence.

With Ian Smith's illegal Unilateral Declaration of Independence in 1965, the stage for the final confrontation was set and the war of liberation was joined. Though the battle was long and bloody, with retribution on both sides, the end of 1979 saw conciliation and the inauguration of a one-man, one-vote democratic society after years of oppression and suppression.

Thus, when the new green, gold, red, and black flag of Zimbabwe was raised at midnight on 17 April, 1980, bitterness was set aside in the joy of nationhood and Robert Mugabe, founding father, began the task of bringing together the many disparate groups, including large minorities like the Ndebele and the European community, as one people building one nation.

The green of the flag represents the land; gold its mineral wealth; red the blood shed for freedom; and black the country's people. To the left is a white triangle that stands for the final peace. On the triangle is The Zimbabwe Bird a representation of eight carved soapstone birds, mounted on stone columns that were found within the ritual enclosure in the ruins of Great Zimbabwe and carried off by art collectors. All but one has since been returned. The red star behind the bird represents Zimbabwe's national hopes.

The name Zimbabwe was taken from *dzimba dzemagwe*, the Shona words for 'big houses of stone', which was the name given to the residences of the Shona royal family.

Similar themes are expressed in the national coat of arms, where the colour green represents the fertility of the land; the wavy blue and white lines, the water which brings prosperity; the rifle and the hoe, the transition from war to peace; the gold and green wreath, the mining and agricultural industries; the star, the hopes for the future tinged with red to recall past bloodshed; the kudu's harmonious colours of black, brown and white, the various ethnic origins of the Zimbabwe people: the earthen mound represents the plants and the clothing which give succour to the people, while the motto emphasises the need for unity and work to preserve the country's hard-won freedom.

Zimbabwe is a democratic republic headed by a President who administers government policy through a ministerial cabinet. General elections are held every five years. The two-house parliament — a senate and a house of assembly — were merged into one chamber in 1990.

Set in south-central Africa, between the Limpopo and Zambezi rivers, Zimbabwe's westernmost corner thrusts into the Caprivi Strip where it meets the borders of Namibia, Angola, Botswana, and Zambia. Bounded by Zambia in the north and north-west, Mozambique in the east, South Africa in the south, and Botswana in the south-west,

Zimbabwe's 390,245 square kilometres, almost the size of California and three times the size of England, lie wholly to the north of the Tropic of Capricorn.

Most of the country consists of a high plateau more than 2,000 feet above sea level. Apart from the Zambezi, Limpopo, and Lake Kariba, its most outstanding physical features are the 350-kilometre-long mountain range in the east and the mineral-rich Great Dyke which runs like a backbone right through the middle of the country, dividing it roughly into the highveld and middleveld.

The largest of the indigenous communities are the Shona and the Ndebele. The others are the Tonga people of the Zambezi Valley, most of whom were displaced and resettled when Lake Kariba was formed, the Sotho, the Hlengwe of the south, and the Vendao, a small group of hunter-gatherers.

The most widely-spoken Bantu languages are Shona and Ndebele but English, which unites all the different people with one common tongue, is the official language.

Today the minority European and Asian communities have joined hands with the indigenous people of Zimbabwe, made up of six main ethnic groups, speaking many dialects, and the past, if not forgotten, is forgiven.

As sunny as their magical land, studded with granite hills, green and fertile plains, high moorlands and craggy, forest-topped mountains, rolling savannah and flowing rivers, the Zimbabwean people are building a society where all are equal and a better quality of life is sought for all.

But with an estimated population of 8.5 million in 1985, and growing yearly by more than 3.5 per cent, there is intense pressure on the government to satisfy expectations, and on demographic and development planners to create housing and employment.

To cope with the migration of rural people to the cities, planners built the satellite city of Chitungiwiza, close to Harare. By 1989 it was the country's third-largest urban conurbation.

Nonetheless, there have been dramatic improvements in social welfare and education, matched by impressive developments in the industrial, agricultural, and tourism sectors.

Since 1980, change has been swift and stunning. More than 5,000 kilometres of smooth two-lane metalled highways and 20,000 kilometres of state-maintained gravel or dirt road link virtually every area of the country. And 60,000 kilometres of rural roads are maintained by local and district authorities.

Major cities and tourist centres are also joined by scheduled daily Air Zimbabwe jet services and frequent passenger trains. Zimbabwe has one of the most developed rail systems in Africa with more than 3,400 kilometres of track.

Though electric locomotives haul freight between Gweru and Harare, and diesels operate over the rest of the system, Zimbabwe still has one of the largest surviving steam networks in the world. The luxurious week-long steam safaris to places like Victoria Falls are a joy for railway enthusiasts the world over. In their majesty, the giant veteran Garratt steam locomotives that roar along the edge of Hwange

Above: Lilac-breasted roller on the banks of the Zambezi River.

Above: Starlings like this are among more than 400 species of bird — both resident and migratory — recorded in Zimbabwe.

National Park match the elephant herds browsing by the line.

For, despite its population pressures, Zimbabwe has one of the finest conservation records in the world. Much of the country — almost 50,000 square kilometres, virtually thirteen per cent of its total land area — is conserved as a wildlife and wilderness estate without equal anywhere else in the world except, perhaps, for its distant north-eastern neighbours, Kenya and Tanzania.

In 1989, there were eleven national parks, fourteen botanical reserves, three botanical gardens, seventeen designated safari areas, six sanctuaries and fifteen recreational parks. In all, these account for 49,780 square kilometres of Zimbabwe's total land area. Farmers and other individuals have also established many private game ranches and wildlife parks. In some safari areas, hunting is allowed such is Zimbabwe's conservation record.

At an average cost of US$600 a day for each individual, plus heavy payments for trophy licences, hunting enables excess wildlife populations to be culled while earning income to meet the increasing overheads incurred by intensive wildlife management and conservation projects.

These wildlife sanctuaries sustain some of the last great concentrations of African wildlife: imperilled elephant and rhino, herds of buffalo and antelope such as the magnificent greater kudu, while Lake Kariba boasts the largest population of Nile crocodile in the world, almost 40,000.

Rich in fable, too, Zimbabwe is the legendary land of Ophir, the ancient country that enriched the kingdoms of Hiram, Solomon, and Sheba with gold and ivory thousands of years ago.

Certainly in the first millennium AD, long before Livingstone's 'discovery', the lower Zambezi was a highway for Arab trade and later for the Portuguese. Like him, these early traders discovered a land blessed with one of the most idyllic climates in the world.

To travel through Zimbabwe is to experience the joy of discovery in one of Africa's — and the world's — great unspoilt tourist attractions. In the vastness of its national parks and game sanctuaries the welcome and the wonder of that Africa which was felt more than a century ago by traders, missionaries, explorers, and adventurers, can be sensed again.

Among them was David Livingstone who was taken by dugout canoe down the swift-flowing Zambezi to the edge of the great falls. Though he had seen 'five columns of vapour rising 250 feet to mingle with the clouds' he was unprepared for the spectacle that greeted him after he stepped ashore on the island that today bears his name.

Africa's fourth-largest and least spoilt river, the Zambezi rises at the start of its 2,700 kilometre journey to the Indian Ocean on the slopes of a small, remote and little-known hill where the Zaire border meets the far north-western corner of Zambia and the easternmost boundary of Angola.

Almost as soon as this nascent, sunbright stream leaps and bounds down the hills it enters Angola. But never Zaire's and not quite Angola's, even though it flows through it for 300 kilometres, this river belongs exclusively in the world's mind to Zambia, Zimbabwe, and Mozambique.

Above: A species of Erythrina tree in Nyanga National Park.

Where it re-enters Zambia, at Angola's Caripande border post, it rages downstream over the Chovuma Falls and through the rapids of the Nyamboma Gorge before slowing down to meander over the Luena Flats, on past Senange to Kazungula where it forms Zimbabwe's northern border with Zambia.

Some eighty kilometres downstream from this point it reaches what, for many explorers and millions of later visitors, is perhaps the summation of a visit to Zimbabwe.

Here the Zambezi, now a solid curtain of water almost two kilometres wide, fragmented only briefly and all too despairingly by three small islands of startling green, thunders over the edge of a sheer, 300 foot precipice.

In spate, between January and April, the Victoria Falls resounds to a deafening anthem of rage as the waters of the Zambezi, pulverized to vapour, rise 1,500 feet into the heavens in an eternal mist for the sun to paint rainbows of celestial glory in the unsullied blue of an azure African sky.

Though undoubtedly this is the apogee of all that occurs during the river's long journey to the sea, it is by no means all that the Zambezi achieves. Downstream from the falls, this great wall of water is captured between 1,000-foot-high cliffs, barely thirty metres apart, and for the next 100 kilometres funnels through the gorge over a series of cataracts in a fury of tormented foam. Where it enters the middle Zambezi Valley, its waters trapped by the Kariba dam, their energy spent, it bellies out to form one of the world's great manmade lakes.

Tamed and under control, its flow regulated, the river passes out into the lower valley which has been transformed by the Kariba hydroelectric scheme into a wilderness without compare.

And where the Zambezi enters Mozambique at Feira, almost at once it forms the second of the great manmade lakes to which it gave birth, Cabora Bassa, almost as long and slender as Lake Kariba.

From this dam it slowly makes its way downstream through Tete, finally to enter the Indian Ocean in a many-fingered delta south of Quelimane and the coastal town of Chinde where, legend says, Solomon and Sheba's envoys came to journey upstream to carry away the treasures of the land of Ophir.

But where Livingstone's statue stands, on a headland above the Devil's Cataract at Victoria Falls, is today undoubtedly the perfect starting point for a *Journey through Zimbabwe*.

2. A Pride of Angels

Just a few paces from the stunted scrub bush of the scorched, dry Kalahari sands that stretch from Botswana to the banks of the Zambezi in north-west Zimbabwe an ancient miracle continues to slake its thirst from the unceasing benediction that has sustained it for thousands of years.

Night and day the solid veil of mist that rises from the chasm of the Victoria Falls pours down on the thick canopy of tangled trees and lianas that cloaks the top of the cliffs opposite. As you step inside the cathedral-like gloom, with its drenched forest floor and rotting underbrush, the sharp African sunlight is suddenly dimmed.

Almost 150 years after David Livingstone — whose fifteen-foot statue now gazes out from a forest glade across this awesome spectacle — first pushed through this rain forest to view the falls, the same timber giants of mahogany, ebony, and fig, together with their symbiotic and parasitic attendants, including rare ferns and mosses, continue to refresh themselves from its soft and nourishing caress.

But where bushbuck and other small game dart suddenly in and out of view, there is none of the still silence usually associated with rain forests, only the continuous thunder of the falls and the perpetual patter of falling rain, ranging in intensity from gentle drizzle to torrential downpour.

The rain forest and Livingstone's larger-than-life bronze likeness, cast in 1954, endure Africa better than he did. Jet travel has placed the continent within reach of everybody. Modern medicine, smooth roads, and luxury hotels have rendered its excitements as safe and enjoyable as they are enthralling.

No such comfort attended the kindly but irascible Scot on his journeys. Eventually both he and his wife, Mary, succumbed to the pestilential fevers that were the great barrier to the continent's development. In fact, Mary, who died of fever in 1862, is buried beside the Zambezi at Shupanga.

Livingstone, who was based in Botswana at the mission station run by Mary's father, Robert Moffat, first saw the Zambezi in 1851. Although he could not have known it then, subsequent explorations have revealed in hidden fossil beds along its banks a near-continuous record of human evolution.

Preserved in the sands and gravels of its shores a treasury of tools made by the early ancestors of modern mankind lay waiting to be uncovered; and not just at Victoria Falls — it is now known that similar fossil beds lie all along the banks of the upper and middle Zambezi. Yet this great river was unknown outside Africa.

One year after crossing the Zambezi's upper stretches, Livingstone pioneered a route to Africa's west coast and back on a journey that took over thirty months.

By September 1855 he was back on the upper reaches of the Zambezi and in November he determined to trace its course to the east coast, and thus open 'God's highway to the sea'. Travelling downstream by dugout canoe, the missionary hoped to pioneer a navigable route along which legitimate traffic would displace the slave trade.

On 15 November, 1855, shafts of gold reflected off the rippling waters, his Makololo crew, glistening backs moving back and forth in

Above: Larger-than-life statue of Scottish missionary David Livingstone, the first known white man to see the Victoria Falls, on 16 November, 1855. It was erected in 1954 to commemorate his 'discovery'.

Previous pages: Herd of sable antelope in the depths of Hwange National Park.

Opposite: The fury and the grandeur of the Victoria Falls where the Zambezi River becomes a curtain of water almost two kilometres wide as it plunges over the basalt lip of a 300 foot precipice. In the last two million years the waters have cut eight falls and are now in the process of carving a ninth. The Devil's Cataract, left, on the Zimbabwe bank of the river is already many feet lower than the other cataracts.

rhythm, beached his canoe on Kalai Island, midstream in the Zambezi, at around sundown. Livingstone camped there overnight before setting off at sunup next morning for the falls, some kilometres downstream, as elephant and other game paraded down to the mainland banks.

Those making the same voyage upstream on one of the regular Zambezi sundowner cruises, drinks to hand, may reflect on the magic of such travel — and compare their experience with what this first European visitor had to contend with.

Negotiating the rapids a little upstream from the falls, his crew landed on the western side of an island that stands at the top of the centre of the precipice. This island now bears his name and marks the Zambian border.

When he reached the edge of its precipice he looked down in awe and humility. On either side of him a solid sheet of water launched itself over the brink. To measure the depth of the falls, the missionary-explorer tied some bullets and a length of calico to a line and lowered it over the edge of the cliff. But it snagged on some rocks about 300 feet below. Livingstone made copious notes of his 'discovery' but no words or statistics can capture or convey the immensity and glory of this natural phenomenon.

Defeated by the rapids at Cabora Bassa, in Mozambique, his mission to trace the Zambezi's course failed. But his discoveries provoked even greater interest in Africa, generally, and in the Zambezi valley in particular.

Not long after this, Thomas Baines, a self-taught artist from King's Lynn, England, accompanied Livingstone on a subsequent expedition to explore the Zambezi in 1857. He was dismissed after an argument but in 1861 he set out again for the Zambezi with hunter and trader James Chapman. They arrived at the falls in July 1862 and Baines spent twelve days sketching and painting them from every angle. His pictures were the first to portray their grandeur and beauty to the rest of the world.

Livingstone believed the falls had arisen because of a sudden and cataclysmic rifting of the earth's surface some time in Africa's ancient past. But in fact they are the result of steady and constant change and not some dramatic reshaping of the landscape.

Twice the height and one and a half times the width of North America's Niagara Falls, the ancestry of this great natural wonder of the world goes back to the age of the dinosaurs 150 million years ago when widespread volcanic activity changed the shape and form of southern Africa and — where the falls now thunder and rage — pushed up a huge slab of basalt.

Between eleven and ten million years ago when the Zambezi is believed to have flowed southward into the Orange River, a gentle uplifting of the earth changed its course to the east and, much later, it began flowing over the basalt plateau.

Slowly, over many thousands of years, the river knifed through the limestone faults in its new bed. Indeed, the present falls are just one of a continuing series that the Zambezi began cutting around two million years ago.

The first of these magnificent falls was formed some eight kilometres

Above: Plaque above the Victoria Falls narrates the history of the 'Mosi-oa-Tunya' — the 'smoke that thunders'.

downstream from the present one. During the millenniums that followed, the Zambezi carved another seven falls, cutting back on its course each time by wearing down a series of east-west fissures, and is now in the process of shaping the ninth.

The volume of the falls varies considerably. At their lowest, between November and December, as little as 20,000 cubic metres of water a minute flow into the gorge below. But when the rains are heavy the flow increases swiftly and dramatically. Between January and April, when they are at their most spectacular, more than 500,000 cubic metres a minute cascade over the edge.

On one occasion in 1958, when the flow reached more that 700,000 cubic metres a minute, the water in the gorge rose sixty feet above its normal flood level, double the depth of the seasonal variation in the water levels.

Bank to bank, the total width of the falls is 1.7 kilometres, with the islands accounting for 400 metres of this distance. The height of the various falls ranges between 327 and 380 feet.

In April, the peak of the flood season, the six falls — Devil's Cataract, Main Falls, Horseshoe Falls, Rainbow Falls, Armchair Falls, and the Eastern Cataract — form the largest curtain of falling water in the world. But in the dry season, between September and November, almost no water plunges over the Rainbow and Armchair Falls and the Eastern Cataract on the Zambian side.

More and more, the Zambezi funnels itself into the narrow Devil's Cataract on the west bank, already worn down many feet below the level of the other falls. The Zambezi is now carving through fissures in Cataract Island. Eventually, many thousands of years from now, a new gorge will follow this line all the way across to Zambia, replacing the present falls.

All that disturbs the natural beauty of this setting — though many will argue that its engineering attributes match the grandeur around it — is the bridge that spans the chasm formed by the previous falls at its narrowest point.

The bridge was placed there at the wish of Cecil Rhodes who envisaged a Cape to Cairo railway as one of the main linchpins in his grand design to colonize Africa. He said the bridge should be built close enough for passengers to see the falls and feel the spray. Although he died in March 1902, two years before the railway reached Victoria Falls in June 1904, preliminary work began in 1903.

This great feat of engineering took fourteen months to complete. Men, equipment, and supplies were moved from one side to the other on a trolley suspended from a cable slung more than 350 feet above the water raging through the gorge below. The breaking point of the cable was fifteen tonnes but when heavy rolling stock was being moved it sagged by as much as twenty-five feet.

Construction of the main girder work, which started on both sides early in 1905, took only nine weeks. So accurate was the engineering that the centre section of the 500-foot arch slotted into place exactly on 2 April, 1905 (the bridge, which carries both the railway and the road, was rehabilitated in 1980). It was opened on 12 September, 1905.

Initially those who crossed the bridge had to pay a ten cent toll to

Above: Masked traditional dancer entertains tourists with folk dance that has its genesis in tribal legends.

Jack Soper who gave up crocodile hunting to become the tollmaster. He was one of the first of those colourful eccentrics whose names stud the early European history of Africa. Another was Pierre Gavuzzi, the first manager of the iron and timber Victoria Falls hotel, raised on stilts to avoid damp and termites, which opened in June 1904. It consisted of twelve single rooms and four doubles, with a dining room and bar. In fact, it was so basic that many preferred to sleep aboard the train parked at the station.

Soon, however, a stream of visitors, mainly the wealthy, aristocratic, and famous, or adventurers, traders, and hunters, were making the long pilgrimage to see this natural marvel and within eight years, overlooking the second gorge and the bridge, a new hotel had taken the place of the first. Now much enlarged and frequently refurbished, the wide, terraced gardens, spacious guest rooms, banqueting hall and original public rooms remain nostalgic reminders of the elegance and grandeur of those early days.

The hotel was given a royal accolade when Britain's King George VI, Queen Elizabeth, and Princess Elizabeth and Princess Margaret, stayed

Overleaf: The constant spray from the Victoria Falls, sometimes rising as high as 1,500 feet, nurtures a unique rain forest on the Zimbabwe side. The road-rail bridge over the Batoka gorge in the foreground was built on the orders of Cecil Rhodes but work only began after his death. It took fourteen months to complete.

Above: Tribal witchdoctor at a traditional African village in Victoria Falls casts charms to divine the future.

there during their visit to Southern Africa in 1947.

Steam still lives on in Zimbabwe and the destination board in the pretty little station near the hotel noting the 2,651 kilometres to Cape Town and the 1,534 kilometres to Beira is a monument to the vast distances that these mammoths of the track used to cover.

Even so, the development of the small and once remote town above the falls as a major tourist destination only really began in the 1960s. Until then, there were just one or two traders selling curios and souvenirs.

But in the last thirty years new hotels, an international airport, and a rapidly-growing shopping centre have replaced the curio stalls. Today most visitors fly into the airport twenty-one kilometres from Victoria Falls town although some still arrive by rail while others journey by road from Zambia and Botswana's nearby Chobe National Park.

Modern hotels and casinos entertain tourists during the evening and the all too brief days are spent exploring the wonders of the falls and the scenic beauty of the Zambezi river.

The falls and the rain forest on its cliffs, are preserved as a 23.4 square kilometre national park. It has also been nominated a World Heritage Site but much depends on Zambia. Next to it, covering 573 square kilometres, is the Zambezi National Park with its elephant and buffalo herds, magnificent sable, impala, and kudu antelope, and myriad other game.

Conscious of the heritage it holds in trust for the world, Zimbabwe's National Parks management has maintained the falls and the rain forest virtually as they were when Livingstone first saw them. Thus the forest and cliffs are preserved in pristine form, apart from some stone steps, built long before it became a national park, which lead down the cliff to provide a close-up view of the Devil's Cataract and the full length of the falls.

Though small in size, this unique sanctuary is rich with wildlife, birdlife, and botanical glories. One of the marvels of Zimbabwe is its butterflies and here yellow pansies, diadem, orange-tips, and many others flit through the forest.

In the trees, and soaring above the falls and the surrounding landscape, bird lovers are able to see the tawny-flanked prinia with its long, slender upstanding tail, blue waxbills, firefinches, mannikins, tchagaras, black-eyed bulbuls, bateleur eagles, Heuglin's robin, the exquisite paradise flycatcher, collared and scarlet-breasted sunbirds, and many others. They feast on the forest's abundant insects. Dragonflies constantly hover over the perpetual pools, particularly in December when they come out in swarms.

One of the most outstanding birds is a rarely seen turaco — the remarkable Livingstone's loerie. If lucky you may see it in distant flight between the treetops or over the gorge. In the shimmering mist its plumage glimmers metallic blue-black against its vivid red flight feathers but closer inspection shows that the upper parts in fact are bright green. With its tapering crest, eyes set within a red, white and black triangle, this turaco is unmistakable.

Disappearing through the sopping undergrowth of leaf litter and rotting twigs at the first footfall of an approaching visitor are skinks and

snakes. More obvious, in some clearings you may come across a dung beetle assiduously rolling a ball of manure across the path. The spoors of bigger denizens are frequently seen: bushbuck, waterbuck, leopard, wart hog, mongoose, and baboon. At night hippo emerge from their pools to wander the open crest of the cliffs, foraging for the lush grasses sustained by the perpetual rain.

Above: Sundowner cruise on the mirror-like waters of the Zambezi above the Victoria Falls.

The real glory of the forest, however, is its plant life — creepers, vines, and giant trees, including the parasitical strangler fig which soon embraces and smothers its host. Among the tangled mass of interwoven trees and lianas are the African mangosteen, an unusual climbing acacia, and the potato creeper which sends out clusters of mauve and yellow flowers remarkably similar to those that bloom on nightshade.

You'll also find the curious spreading Cape fig, a large leafy tree whose fruit sprouts only from leafless branches or straight from its main trunk. Elsewhere, small trees and shrubs are festooned with the brown and green flowers of the creeping flame lily and in small crevices in the cliffs of the falls aloes maintain a tenacious toe hold.

Where the forest becomes more luxuriant, the trees are embraced by many creepers and the undergrowth is rich in ferns. Between October and December the large vivid-red flowers of the blood lily seem to set the undergrowth on fire.

And everywhere, among the mahoganies and the ebonies, false date palms, cape figs, and waterberries, the creepers and the lianas, flourishes a profusion of orchids.

Above: One of many palm-studded islands in the wide reaches of the Zambezi that Livingstone encountered on his canoe voyage to Victoria Falls.

Most visitors view the falls for the first time on foot, walking through the forest from Livingstone's statue where there is a viewpoint of the boiling fury of the Devil's Cataract. The statue, 'erected to the memory of their distinguished countryman through the united efforts of the Caledonian Society' was unveiled on 6 August, 1954, by Livingstone's nephew, Howard Unwin Moffat, who served as Prime Minister of Rhodesia from 1927 to 1935.

The impressive likeness, commemorating Livingstone's life from 19 March, 1815, until 1 May, 1873, was finally raised due to the untiring efforts of William Lowe, who served as Chairman of the Livingstone Memorial Committee from its inception in 1926 until his death in 1935.

On 16 November, 1955, fifteen months later, another ceremony took place which was commemorated by a plaque, unveiled by Lord Llewellin, Governor-General of the Federation of Rhodesia and Nyasaland, and dedicated by the Archbishop of Central Africa, Edward Francis Paget.

The inscription reads: 'On the occasion of the centenary of David Livingstone's discovery of the Victoria Falls men and women of all races in, and from all parts of, the federation of Rhodesia and Nyasaland assembled solemnly to dedicate themselves to carry on the high Christian aims and ideals which inspired David Livingstone in his mission here.'

As you follow the path winding in and out of the forest, perhaps descending the steps to the lower viewpoint, you see the falls from

Opposite: Leopard in Hwange National Park. They kill anything from small rodents to medium and large gazelle and antelope. They even eat fish and come readily to carrion.

Above: Yellow-billed hornbill, one of many hornbill species found in Zimbabwe.

many perspectives — and the more you look and listen, the more the sound and the fury mesmerises. In sequence, one by one along the path, you come to clifftop glades that overlook their own particular spectacle: Cataract Island, the Main Falls, Livingstone Island, Horseshoe Falls, Rainbow, and Armchair Falls — none ever much more than sixty metres distant; but views into the bottom of the gorge itself are rare, the pounding spray too great to see much anyway.

And although the constant downpour soaks you to the skin, who but the meanest spirit would scorn rain from a sky of purest blue by sheltering under an umbrella or raincoat?

Finally, standing under the warm sun on the precipitous edge of Danger Point, there's a panoramic view of the great sheet of water which has travelled 1,400 kilometres. It seems almost to pause as it gathers itself together and then, in a stunning increase of tempo as if scenting liberation, hurls itself into the abyss — only to be as suddenly captured, choked, and constrained in the narrow neck of the Boiling Pot.

Nothing, you may think, could survive this seething maelstrom of malevolent energy as wave after pounding wave is stirred by incredible eddies and whirlpools before breaking free from its rocky prison to begin the 100-kilometre race down Batoka Gorge to Lake Kariba.

Yet amazingly this is now the locale for what is probably the most perilous river-running enterprise in the world, an experience that would have turned Davy Crockett grey before his time. It makes anything produced by Hollywood seem like a peaceful river cruise. Early each morning between May and December those in search of heart-stopping adventure make their way down the cliffside to launch their rubber dinghy into the maniacal waters of the Zambezi.

For twenty-three kilometres the adrenalin doesn't stop pumping as the dinghy plunges in and out of thirteen of the Zambezi's most formidable grade eight to ten rapids, with their uncharted potholes and whirlpools, hidden rocks and boulders. Enthusiasts, admittedly sometimes a little pale under their tan, rate it the world's ultimate white-water rafting adventure.

When the sport was pioneered in this section of the Zambezi in the 1980s it was thought that crocodiles — something that river-runners don't have to contend with in other parts of the world — could not survive in such turbulent water. But since then they have been added to the list of uncounted perils. And even when the run is over and you step ashore, breathlessly alive, you still have to find your way up the 1,000-foot cliffs of the Batoka Gorge.

Many prefer, and who can blame them, to take the twenty-minute 'Flight of Angels' which provides a memorable panorama of the upstream river and its many islands, and the fearful constriction of the downstream gorge. Apart from the gorges and mountains of the Himalaya, nothing so well evokes an awareness of nature's infinite majesty — nor emphasizes so sharply the insignificance of mankind.

On the scenic Zambezi Drive which circles the rain forest there's another reminder of the omnipotent power of nature: a giant, 1,500-year-old baobab tree with a trunk that is sixty metres thick — large enough to garage a car within.

A century and a half ago all this area was under the sway of the Makololo, a breakaway splinter group of the Zulu who dominated, briefly, the indigenous Leyas, Tongas, and Subiyas of the region.

In the evening, in the boma of an indigenous craft village, entertainers demonstrate the vigour and spirit of Zimbabwean cultures in dance, mime, and comedy. Under the pin-bright stars of the southern skies, the drums pound out the pulsating rhythm of the Zulu war dances and circumcision rituals. The accompaniment, the familiar, reedy soprano salutes of young maidens, echoes with the soul of timeless Africa. And the stirring rallying call of a high-pitched fanfare from a kudu horn trumpet expresses the joy of a people exulting in the triumph of their warriors.

The light catches in the eyes of a pretty young African girl, white diamonds set in ebony, and their hidden depths sparkle with fires that were lit long before Livingstone made his way downstream on the river that murmurs in the dark just beyond the village.

Perhaps, too, the display is not something pulled from the past merely for the tourist audience but a celebration of the heritage and

Above: Elephant-watching tourists in the tangled scrub woodland of 573-square-kilometre Zambezi National Park.

Opposite: A pack of dwarf mongoose take the sun outside their rocky lair. These small and friendly diminutives make ideal pets. In the wild they move around in packs of up to fifteen.

Above: Vervet monkey steals a drink.

Right: Female greater kudu in Hwange National Park.

freedom so recently reclaimed.

Sadly, some of the physical scars of the 1965-79 liberation war — including the ruins of the Elephant Hills Club with its panoramic view over the Zambezi and a fenced section of the Zambezi National Park that warns of mines where today elephant roam, seemingly without injury — still remained in 1989. But nothing mars the glory of the Zambezi upstream from the falls.

In some places the river is more than two kilometres wide and it was at one of these points just after the Second World War that the Solent flying boats of Britain's Imperial Airways landed on their leisurely five-day journey from Southampton, across the Mediterranean, via Cairo and Khartoum on the Nile, Lake Victoria, through the Zambezi, to Vaal Dam in South Africa. In December, 1982, British Airways placed a memorial on the former landing stage along the river banks where their 'jungle junction' operated and the small airline buildings are now a fishing camp.

Those who wish to discover more of the Zambezi's magic can explore the eighty kilometres of river between Kazungula, on the Botswana and Zimbabwe borders with the Caprivi strip, and the falls on a canoe safari — shooting a series of rapids at Katombora, Sansimba, and finally Kandahar, during three days and nights of adventure in raw, and totally unspoilt Africa.

Until recently only a handful of people, including Livingstone, had ever ventured this journey which combines long, idyllic stretches of calm water and palm-covered white sand islands with the nerve-tingling thrill of white-water canoeing.

For those who prefer something less strenuous and more relaxing, upstream fishing and wildlife lodges offer a touch of adventure with serenity and luxury in uncrowded intimacy. None cater for more than eighteen guests at a time and one only accommodates a maximum of six guests.

Those short on time might simply choose the cruise upstream to Kandahar Island in the pale blush of dawn for a champagne breakfast and the crisp promise of newborn day as the rising sun strikes through the tall palms.

They say that only vervet monkeys live on Kandahar and Palm Island where giant palms flourish, but elephant periodically swim across to seek out the palm fruit.

For one tourist, drifting slowly on a sundown cruise to Kandahar and Palm Islands opposite Kalai Island, where Livingstone camped, recalls memories of a morning's cruise on another African river, the Nile, downstream from Murchison Falls, that was made seventeen years before. The images of past and present are in balance. Unlike the great waterways in the west of the continent, the African pageant on these banks remains unspoiled and primaeval. He says it is as if time has stood still.

The great river seems almost motionless. Indeed, the wind on its surface makes it appear to flow upstream. But out in the mainstream there is a brisk chop and here and there the deceptively-gentle eddies of treacherous whirlpools and hidden sandbanks. A lone, almost forlorn figure stands on the distant Zambian shore.

In a deep pool nearby, a sounder of hippos break surface, indistinguishable from the rocks that surround them save for the endless fidget of their ears and the swivelling intensity of their periscope stare.

Cormorants, wings extended, stand in frozen silhouette, like a taxidermist's window-display, on the stump of a dead tree against the red orb of the setting sun.

Egrets flutter on the banks, alternating between piggy-back rides on their symbiotic hosts, the buffalo, and a final sundown display of formation flying.

Almost imperceptibly, the surface close to the bank is silently broken by the swirl of a Nile crocodile taking to the water. At one stage the Zambezi's crocodile population was seriously threatened but it is now being extensively managed. Crocodile farms are exploiting their meat and leather and these great saurians are being reintroduced to the Zimbabwe reaches of the river.

There is magic in this river, the Zambezi, the magic of unchanging Africa and the wonder of its banks crowded with elephant, buffalo, and antelope come down to water and its bottom-trotting hippo and lurking crocodile, all revealed against the late afternoon or early morning light.

Some forty-two kilometres south of Victoria Falls lies another magical place, one of Zimbabwe's least spoilt wildlife sanctuaries. Sandwiched to the west and east between the Matetsi Safari Area, Kazuma Pan

Above: Oribi in a thicket. Shy and easily startled these small antelope are rarely seen.

Above: Shot into limbo by early sports hunters, white rhino have now been reintroduced to Hwange National Park.

National Park's 312 square kilometres of Kalahari grasslands draw great flocks of waterfowl to its many seasonal flood pans.

The park, circled by dense teak forests, is alive with many prides of lion, rare antelope such as the gemsbok, tsesseby, and oribi, buffalo; and endangered species like black rhino, the Disney-like bat eared fox, Cape hunting dog, and elephant. It is also an ideal habitat for the fleet-footed cheetah, fastest land animal in the world.

No roads link this remote and enchanting wilderness with the rest of the country. The only way in is across country by four-wheel drive, preferably with the tour organization that runs a luxury camp based at one of the permanent waterholes.

Nights spent here talking quietly around the camp fire to the sounds of the African night induce euphoria — unless the spell is broken by the roar of lion close by or the sawing grunt of leopard.

Left: Greater kudu at one of the permanent water pans in Hwange National Park's 14,000-square-kilometre wilderness. Weighing between 270 and 320 kilos, greater kudu sport what are perhaps the most magnificent horns in the animal kingdom, and have fewer stripes on the flank than the lesser kudu. The record trophy measures a fraction under 1.8 metres (six feet).

No doubt, some rough trail leads east from Kazuma Pan across the former farmlands of the Matetsi Safari Area to the railroad halt of that name on the side road to Nantwich and Robin's Camp in Hwange National Park. These were abandoned because of poor soil and erratic rainfall, but since Independence the Matetsi's 2,955 square kilometres have become Zimbabwe's major wildlife hunting preserve. The magnificent sable, elephant, and buffalo trophies taken by clients hunting with one of the many professional safari hunting companies that operate in this area have become an important source of foreign exchange for the country.

Most visitors, however, drive directly from Victoria Falls along the modern highway through the colliery town of Hwange, and then take the right turn to the Hwange Safari Lodge and Hwange National Park's Main Camp.

The arrow-straight road runs through what is basically a featureless flatland of mopane. Unusually for Africa, there is no great panorama. Indeed, the impression is that of travelling through a single, infinite avenue of trees where the beautiful colours of fall and spring meld in a sonnet of red, russet, ochre, and green. Some green foliage, in particular, is startling in its intensity, almost phosphorescent. Briefly glimpsed through breaks in the mopane bush are the fascinating ridgebacks of kopjes and inselbergs rising out of the semi-arid landscape.

But although panoramas are rare and fleeting in these low flatlands, the railway line and telegraph poles are the only indications of

Above: Male and female sable near Matetsi Safari Area. The coat of the much larger males is almost pure black while that of the female is a dark reddish-brown. Sable prefer woodlands to open plains.

development. Soon, however, the road climbs gently over a low pass to reveal the incongruous sight of Hwange, a vast area of underground and opencast collieries with all the attendant scars of industrial development — cooling towers, slag heaps, a land stained black, a countryside eroded by mankind's exploitation.

If the land carries scars, so do the hearts of many of the people who live there. In 1972 the town's Number Two colliery was the scene of one of the world's worst coal pit disasters when 427 miners were killed by an underground explosion.

Since 1980 the town has grown considerably and many new mines have been developed to exploit the mineral wealth beneath the surface, including copper and tin. Opencast coal mining has also been developed in recent years.

Although it was known by the odd name of Wankie until Independence, the town's name derives from Hwange, one of the old chiefs of the Rozvi tribe who made this their homeland.

If a necessary blot on the landscape — and necessary it must be since it is also the dynamo that drives economic development — the despoliation is visible only briefly, before the road curves through Hwange's residential area.

On top of a lone hill above the town sits a comfortable English-style hotel — it takes its name from the massive old giant that sits on its brow — famous for its bacon sandwiches and its incredible views far south-east. The Baobab Hotel is something of a Mecca for steam enthusiasts. The hill commands an impressive viewpoint for pictures of the Beyer-Garratt steam locomotives rolling their way to the Hwange colliery yards and north-west to Victoria Falls.

Many African *aficionados* will find the images hereabouts schizophrenic, out of tune with their cherished images of a Utopian wilderness land, but within minutes of leaving it is no longer a question of comparing that natural architectural masterpiece, the termite hill, with cooling towers and mineheads.

The main road crosses communal lands with many neatly-thatched homesteads — each dominated by a main hut circled by several smaller huts in a fenced compound where the livestock is penned at night — and Africa stretches before you again in all its arid, untouched infinity.

The western civilization laid on Eastern Africa is only a veneer. In Zimbabwe it is thicker, more visible and durable, especially in such ugly places as Hwange.

But the cultures and landscapes outside the European influence remain wholly African. This land where the termite hills gradually become bigger and bigger, massive mounds and conical peaks, is too dry to be of any value except to those who have survived centuries in Africa; a land that looks too mean to be cherished and too harsh to be exploited.

Yet, though its owners may be several rungs down the economic ladder, the neatness of their homes shows the level of pride they feel even though theirs is a subsistence existence.

The old road to Bulawayo — two tyre-tread-wide strips of tarmac — constantly crisscrosses the new until, finally, you turn right to Hwange National Park's main entrance down a road lined with stands of sap-green trees.

Opposite: Deep in the heart of Hwange National Park, southern Africa's largest game park, majestic elephant come to water watched by fascinated guests on a game walk.

Left: Lethal puff-adder, one of the most dangerous snakes in the world. Sluggish and slow moving they strike swiftly when disturbed and inject venom deep into the victim. Death is slow and extremely painful.

In the nineteenth century it was the royal hunting reserve of King Mzilikazi and his successor Lobengula. But blood soaked deep into the sparse soils as the first white hunters and settlers slaughtered its wildlife by the thousand, leaving an empty, useless wasteland, denuded of wildlife, unfit for farming.

There are two distinct geographic zones to the park, neither of them able to support viable agriculture. The flora of the well-drained northern area, part of the Zambezi watershed, is dominated by mopane and mixed terminalia distinctly different from the rest. Elsewhere the Kalahari scrublands, covered with stunted, scattered woodlands of teak and umtshibi trees, drain into Botswana's Makgadkadi Depression. This habitat is characterised by many marshy depressions, vleis, and fragile open grasslands on shallow soils.

Declared a game reserve in 1928, founding warden Ted Davison walked almost everywhere to survey his new domain. There was extremely little wildlife. The early hunters and later poachers had reduced the once-teeming elephants to fewer than 1,000 and the rhinoceros, both black and white, had been exterminated.

The poorly-drained Kalahari sands with their relatively low rainfall were unable anyway to support permanent large wildlife populations. After the rains the seasonal pans and fossil river lines held water all too briefly and only occasionally did any large numbers migrate into the region.

Water, Davison realised, was the critical key. During the years that followed he drilled several boreholes and created sixty new pans, linked to the seasonal pans that already existed. Slowly, the animals, particularly elephant and buffalo, began to return.

Close to half a century later, Hwange faced another, different crisis — too many elephants. They had risen to more than 20,000 and in their wake left fallen woods and fragile, overgrazed grasslands. Hwange's existence was threatened. Wildlife authorities culled at least 5,000 to

Opposite: Thatched dining room of Sable Valley, one of Touch the Wild's secret retreats deep in the bush.

bring the population to between 12,000 and 15,000, the maximum that Hwange can support without damage.

Water remains the single most important management factor in Hwange's continued existence — absolutely vital to the survival of perhaps Africa's largest single concentration of the threatened elephant.

The constant maintenance of these artificial but natural-looking water pans, complete with resident hippo and predatory crocodiles, has been the major factor in sustaining this ecological treasury. Without them, Hwange would return to the empty wasteland it once was.

Much of the park is inaccessible simply because the number of roads has been deliberately restricted and off the road driving is prohibited. Consequently its wildlife lives an existence untrammelled by intrusive mankind.

But where you can travel — in the west, centre, and to the east — three well-developed safari circuits, served by more than 450 kilometres of well-maintained roads, richly reward the visitor.

Thatched self-service chalets, cottages, and luxury lodges along with caravan and camp sites are available at Main Camp, the park's immaculately-maintained headquarters, complete with supermarket and a pub, the 'Waterbuck's Head'. There are similar self-service facilities at Robin's Camp in the west, named after the rancher who developed the area as a private game sanctuary.

Two special camps — Sinametella and Nantwich — are made up of luxury lodges but apart from these and the comfortable viewing platforms raised by some waterholes there is no other permanent development.

Thus Hwange, with its great wildlife populations, remains one of the most unspoilt wildlife sanctuaries in the world where the varied geography encourages a meeting of two distinct faunal groups. The animals of the arid Kalahari intermingle with species suited to less-harsh, less-arid habitats in great concentrations.

More than 100 species of mammals, including growing numbers of rhino, 15,000 buffalo, 3,000 zebra, 3,000 giraffe, and sixteen of the thirty-three species of southern African antelope — among them 6,000 impala, 5,000 kudu, 2,000 sable, wildebeest, topi, hartebeest, tsesseby, roan and gemsbok — have made Hwange and the surrounding areas their home.

Such numbers attract many predators: lion and leopard, an occasional cheetah, abundant spotted hyena and a rare brown hyena or two. There are also more than 400 species of bird.

An afternoon on a viewing platform at one of the waterholes, strong cool winds alternating with moments of fiery stillness, is unforgettable. Friendly hornbills, unused to mankind and unsuspecting, cocking their head left, then right, with beady-eyed curiosity, perch within hand's reach.

Above the waterhole, where two inert forms lie half-submerged on the sandy bank, a bateleur eagle circles on a Kalahari thermal, its wings a model of futuristic aerodynamics.

All the world stands still. Only the lyrical sounds of silence — the soughing of the wind, the rustle of the sand, and the whirr of a hovering dragonfly — move the clock forward.

Tails erect, a family of unheeding wart hog trot with brisk military

Above: Young martial eagle. Its underside has yet to assume its characteristic adult colour when it becomes flecked with large brown spots.

Previous pages: Sable at sundown.

Above: Nature's original delta-wing, the bateleur eagle's erratic, stiff-winged flight earned it its name — from the French word for 'tumbler'.

gait towards the waterhole only for the leading patriarch to suddenly skitter and brake on his rear legs as, now nervous, he scents the presence of the two crocodiles.

The wart hog skirt the recumbent forms. Now a magnificent sable bull strolls gracefully in to suddenly freeze as it comes within two metres of the crocodiles whose positions have changed imperceptibly.

As the afternoon wears on, one of the crocodiles, restlessly hungry, moves with sudden sluggishness into the water where through the rest of the long hot day it drifts first to one point and then another. But it is destined to stay hungry. Today there will be no privileged witness to the great life and death pageant of the wilderness.

Outside the park, on the road from the Main Camp to Hwange Airport where lion sometimes block the runway, the land is still filled with game; an elephant in a waterhole by the roadside, giraffe crossing unconcerned by the traffic. All seem blessed by the benevolence of this environment where the birds are uncannily tame and only natural predators spook the game.

On a salient to the north, the 148 square kilometres of Hwange Safari Estate, a private game reserve, offer a similar wildlife spectacle. Pampered guests at the luxurious Hwange Safari Lodge don't have to move farther than the bar or their bedroom for close-up encounters with herds of elephant that sometimes number 100 or more, buffalo, sable, impala, and the creatures, wild and wonderful, great and small, which make Hwange a wildlife destination unmatched in southern Africa.

Three luxury retreats in the reserve are run by Touch the Wild's highly idiosyncratic Alan Elliott, his wife, Scotty, and his mother. The bars don't stock cigarettes, the swimming pools are fenced — to avoid toddlers falling in but there's no gate so guests have to climb over — and the animals come before the guests.

An expert in bushcraft who can unfailingly track the spoor of any animal for kilometre after kilometre, Elliott, an experienced after dinner raconteur, confesses his inability to maintain accounts.

His sole passion is Hwange's wildlife. He constantly plants grass to create lawns around the guest rooms of his 'secret valley' lodges and just as constantly the animals uproot it. But he refuses to fence the would-be lawns. 'This place belongs to the animals.'

At sundown, after the scorching daytime heat, the temperature drops dramatically in minutes, often to well below freezing, chilling evidence that despite the thick woodlands this land is held in bondage by the sands of the Kalahari.

On a still and breathless late afternoon, as the sun's shadows lengthen over the place known as Sable Valley, a tusker trumpets herald of its approach to water where a group of white-chested marabou stork, black shrouds on their back, stand motionless like pallbearers drawn to attention for a funeral.

Hwange imprints its memories not only on the mind but on the soul.

3. The Place of Slaughter

From the top of a granite whaleback in the Matobo Hills south of Zimbabwe's second-largest city, Bulawayo, the eye scans across a world in tortured disarray. The ravaged scenery stretches in every direction — a land of tumultuous disorder laid out, it seems, to the gargantuan design of a strange, alien mind.

Spread across more than 3,000 square kilometres, rising serried ridge upon serried ridge far beyond the horizon, these granite hills and cliffs have been sculpted into spires and battlements, towers and turrets, embrasures and fortresses by aeons of wind and rain, sun and erosion.

In the last century the invincible grandeur of these tormented, crenellated citadels of rock made a profound impression on three men of absolute power whose fates were interwoven. The destinies of two drew them together in final confrontation in the last decade of the nineteenth century. And the blood spilled in that outcome seeped into the soil to nourish the seedbed of nationalism which ninety years later gave birth to Zimbabwe.

The first of these three, Mzilikazi, a scion of Matshobana, head of the Khumalo Zulu clan which was finally subordinated by Shaka Zulu, was born around 1795. His father was killed by the rival Zwide clan. But after Shaka defeated the Zwide in 1820 he confirmed Mzilikazi as clan chief, asking only for tribute as token of the clan's allegiance.

Later, when Mzilikazi defied Shaka, the Zulu king sent an army to bring him to heel. They were repulsed at first only for the Khumalo to be cut down in a second raid during which Mzilikazi and a handful of supporters fled.

They regrouped themselves into a force of some strength and over the years, as they slowly made their way north from the Vaal river, fighting all those they came across, Mzilikazi absorbed many of the warriors he conquered into his army, which came to be known as the Ndebele, and thus consolidated his power.

Eventually Mzilikazi settled at Kuruman where the missionary Robert Moffat befriended him. But under constant threat from the Afrikaner voortrekkers advancing across the country, the king decided to move on to new lands.

He crossed the Limpopo and travelled north where he first saw these fantastic formations. Overwhelmed by their grandeur, 'The Great Elephant, Great Mountain, Son of the Sun, God of Cattle and Men', subdued the local tribes and established a new capital, Mhlahlandlela, at their southern base. He named the range *Amatobo*, the Ndebele word for 'bald-heads'.

The Ndebele built upon and reinforced the Zulu tradition of kingship. Mzilikazi placed his wives and trusted *induna*, chiefs, in the villages and settlements that were scattered throughout the kingdom.

His authority was supreme. With a brief, dismissive wave of the hand he condemned those who unwittingly gave offence, or were suspected of disloyalty. Many died in this place.

Yet his hospitality to Moffat and his family, and to the first European hunters and adventurers in search of game trophies, gold and diamonds, was as generous as his welcome was warm. Indeed, when the German Edward Mohr travelled through Matabeleland he reckoned that a foreigner was 'just as safe and his property just as secure as in the

Previous pages: Among the world's oldest rocks, the granite Matobo Hills form a 3,000-square-kilometre landscape of tumultuous disorder.

On the plaque:

BULAWAYO
THE PLACE OF SLAUGHTER

Formerly the royal kraal of LOBENGULA, King of the Matabele & overlord of all the tribes in S. RHODES. A. Messrs. Rudd, Maguire & Thompson, emissaries of RHODES, obtained from LOBENGULA in 1888 a concession of mineral rights which became the pivot of RHODES' famous CHARTER. In 1893 the Matabele-resenting the pressure of British occupation which interfered with their freedom to prey on their neighbours, the Mashona-challenged the white settlers. DR JAMESON & his volunteers drove them back & hoisted the British Flag on the site of the royal kraal, where Government House now stands. (LOBENGULA became a fugitive & died near the Shangani River). In 1896 the Matabele rebelled, but after some months of fighting, RHODES, going unarmed among them, persuaded their Chiefs to accept a lasting peace. The railway reached here in 1897.

Above: Commemorative plaque marks the site of Lobengula's royal kraal, Bulawayo — meaning 'Place of Slaughter' — which was razed by Dr. Leander Starr Jameson, Rhodes's lieutenant, in November 1893. Lobengula fled to die a lonely death of smallpox far from home.

best-governed countries in Europe'.

In 1855, Mzilikazi gave Moffat permission to found the first Christian mission north of the Limpopo and in 1859 showed the missionary's son John Moffat, and his colleague William Sykes, the village of Inyati, 'place of buffaloes', some sixty kilometres north-east of the King's kraal. It was here during Christmas of that year that the two opened their mission.

Towards the end, however, burdened with gout and dropsy, Mzilikazi sought more and more the peace and quiet of his beloved Matobo Hills to commune with the ancestral spirits that the Ndebele believed reposed among them.

It was there, at his favourite sanctuary, Emanxiweni, that he died on 5 September, 1868. His body was taken in stealth, at night, back to the royal kraal at Mhlahlandlela where his death was announced four days later. Guarded by his twelve senior wives, he lay in state for two months before his burial on 2 November at Ntumbane in the Matobo Hills.

In 1941, the Bulawayo Rotary Club raised an imposing memorial on the site of Mzilikazi's royal kraal, twenty-five kilometres from the present capital, where he held his *indaba*, council, under the shade of an umgugutu tree which has since died. The inscription reads:

'Mzilikazi, son of Shobana, King of the Amandebele. All the mountain fell down on 5th September, 1868. All nations acclaim the son of Shobana! Bayete!'

Because it was uncertain whether his first-born son, Nkulumana, was alive, the installation of his second son, Lobengula, was delayed for sixteen months. Even then, the successor had to fight many fierce battles against other contenders to establish his supremacy. But from the outset the new *inkosi* accorded the Europeans, a number of whom lived within the royal kraal or who had built permanent homes in the area, an equal welcome.

Ten of them, including the Reverend Thomas Morgan Thomas, one of Moffat's colleagues, were invited to his coronation which began on 22 January, 1870. They watched as thousands of warriors who had travelled to Lobengula's home at Utjotjo escorted him into the royal kraal at Mhlahlandlela where the ceremonies continued for several days. Lobengula was then thirty-four.

Some Europeans even served as aides, taking down Lobengula's notes for agreements and letters. He was particularly close to the hunter Frederick Courtney Selous until the two fell out in a dispute over the killing of hippos which the Ndebele, who called them 'sea cows', revered.

In the early part of his reign Lobengula adopted a version of European dress, a sailor's striped short and cord trousers, and he commissioned Harry Grant, an old hunter, and his friend John Halyett (known to the Ndebele as Johnny Mubi), to build him a thatched stone building in the style of a Flemish farmhouse. In this palace, before a huge packing case which served as a table, seated on a leather 'throne', its back decorated with a crown, Lobengula held court and entertained his European guests in good humour.

But with the arrival of a British government expedition under Captain Robert Patterson in 1877 seeking free movement throughout Matabeleland, Lobengula's attitude underwent a profound change. He abandoned European ways and went back to his own culture.

Ten years later, as European prospectors and adventurers continued to flood into his country, Lobengula — writing from his new capital of Gubulawayo (Ndebele for the 'place of slaughter') so named to commemorate his victorious battles — complained in a letter to British officials in South Africa that 'the white people . . . come in here like wolves without my permission and make roads to my country. . . . Today is peace but I don't know what tomorrow may bring.'

None of this escaped the attention of Cecil Rhodes who had amassed one of the world's greatest fortunes since he landed in South Africa eighteen years earlier (the year of Lobengula's coronation). Matabeleland had long been the key to his grand design for a British empire in Africa.

The first stage of his strategy was to send a delegation to Bulawayo to negotiate a concession with Lobengula and the Ndebele which would allow the company to operate in Matabeleland.

Above: Memorial raised in 1941 by Bulawayo Rotarians to Mzilikazi, founder of the Ndebele people, on the spot where he built his royal kraal. The inscription ends with the traditional Zulu salute for a fallen king, 'Bayete!'

Old friends also contributed to Lobengula's betrayal, including Moffat's son, John, who lied about the terms of the agreement. On the strength of Moffat's explanation Lobengula put his seal, that of the elephant, to it. Though he later discovered the ruse and repudiated the concession, it was too late. On the strength of this 'agreement', Rhodes established the British South Africa Company.

Yet Lobengula still extended courtesy and protection to many Europeans. In August 1889, Harry Vaughan Williams, nineteen, a young medical student, dined with the king in his stone house on the site where Bulawayo State House now stands. It was filled with the king's treasure.

Two months later, on 29 October, 1889 — only days after Lobengula told Dr. Leander Starr Jameson, Rhodes's emissary to Bulawayo, 'no more lies, I must see Rhodes himself' — Queen Victoria signed the Company's charter and sealed the downfall of Lobengula and the Ndebele nation.

When news of the charter was carried to Lobengula by a detachment of the Royal Horse Guards the king was still amenable enough to take part in the race meeting that was staged to celebrate the event. He entered his own horses in the Gubulawayo Handicap and the Zambezi Plate.

But it was the end of happiness. The following year Rhodes despatched a mercenary army to annexe Mashonaland as the first stage in the overthrow of the Ndebele. They established four forts — Fort Tuli, on the southernmost border, and then marched north-east to set up Fort Victoria, now Masvingo, Fort Charter, and finally Fort Salisbury where they raised the flag on 12 September, 1890.

Three years later, in July, 1893, without provocation, BSAC soldiers attacked a Ndebele attachment which Jameson had summoned to Fort Victoria, massacring between thirty and fifty warriors. Within fourteen weeks, on 4 November, the company flag fluttered from a tree over the smouldering ashes of the royal kraal in Bulawayo and Lobengula was on the run northwards.

Although for many years afterwards the Ndebele clung to the belief that Lobengula was alive, the king is thought to have died of smallpox near Kamativi in February, 1894.

Lobengula left behind, unharmed, two Europeans who had settled in his capital some years before; his advisor and letter writer William Filmer Usher, a member of the Salvation Army, who had been there for ten years, and James Fairbairn, who had arrived twenty-one years earlier and had obtained a gold mining concession from the king.

Now hundreds more poured in, spurred by Rhodes's promises and his vision of a new El Dorado. The European settlement that rose swiftly from the ashes of the Ndebele capital was soon moved five kilometres away. But Rhodes ordered Jameson to build a rondavel on the spot where the kraal had stood.

The new town's streets were extremely wide, broad enough to allow a full team of oxen, twenty-four pairs, to make a 180 degree turn. Fast-growing trees, particularly jacaranda, were planted along each side to create avenues of leafy shade as brick and stone buildings for houses, shops, and bars, began to rise everywhere. Sports fields were cultivated

Above: Cooling towers in the background, the wide, tree-lined streets of Bulawayo, capital of Matabeleland create a city of the twenty-first century. The streets were designed so that a team of sixteen oxen could turn full-circle. Today they ensure abundant car parking space.

for soccer, cricket, and rugby, even a racecourse.

On 1 June, 1894, only seven months after the flag was raised, Jameson stood on the steps of the settlement's first hotel, Maxim's (it no longer exists but a bronze plaque marks the spot) opposite what is now City Hall and declared: 'It is my job to declare this town open, gentlemen, I don't think we want any talk about it. I make the declaration now. There is plenty of whisky and soda inside, so come in.'

Eight months later the population had risen to more than 1,500. Most wanted land — land to settle and farm, or to prospect for the tantalizing riches that the BSAC and Rhodes promised lay beneath the surface.

To provide this, Rhodes appointed a 'Land Commission' which swiftly delineated 10,500 square kilometres of arid, infertile land as the boundaries of a Matabele reserve and expropriated the rest as company land to be sold or otherwise exploited.

But land had to be worked and so began the system of 'forced labour'. To coerce both Ndebele and Shona to work as farmhands and in other menial capacities, a hut tax was introduced. But the Ndebele were not aquiescent.

In April, 1896, between 12,000 and 15,000 Ndebele warriors laid siege to the new town and its 1,500 or so citizens retreated into a laager which was encircled on three sides. The Ndebele left the road south open — no doubt hoping to induce the settlers to leave. The settlers did not retreat. Nor did the Ndebele attack.

Instead, the beleaguered settlers dug a well and the British Government hurriedly deployed troops along this route. By early June a force of more than 3,000 soldiers, BSAC police, and armed volunteers was camped within the laager. The British reprisal was savage and the Ndebele retreated to their stronghold, among the ancestral spirits that reside in the Matobo Hills, to continue the fight.

Their resistance was so stern — and so effective — that Rhodes, under critical pressure in South Africa and abroad, sent the Zulu linguist and local administrator, J. P. Richardson, at great risk to arrange an *indaba* to discuss peace. On 21 August, 1896, accompanied by a friend, a reporter for *The Times* of London, and an interpreter, he rode out to talk to six of the Ndebele's senior *induna*, chiefs, at the place now known as Fort Usher, where William Usher had established a trading post, just a few kilometres to the east of the Matobo Hills. (Later, Lord Baden-Powell decided to build a fort on the spot and, inspired by his scouting expeditions into the hills, conceived the idea of the Boy Scout movement.)

It was during this meeting that Rhodes was shown Mzilikazi's tomb — a natural cave where the body had been placed in a sitting position looking out over the forbidding grandeur of the Matobo Hills. It had been desecrated and he gave orders for it to be restored, and started thinking of his own burial place in these granite hills.

Rhodes held three more meetings, the last two with Lord Grey, who had replaced Jameson as the new administrator of 'southern Rhodesia', and in the settlement reached on 21 October, 1896, conceded much, restoring some of the lands and agreeing to a degree of Ndebele autonomy.

The immediate beneficiary, however, was Bulawayo. Its elevation to a municipality the following year on 27 October coincided with the arrival of the railway from Mafeking. Water supplies and electricity services soon followed and its future was assured.

Now, its population around half a million people, Zimbabwe's second-largest city and its major industrial centre, with its wide, handsome tree-lined streets, and pleasant suburbs, spreads out across the level plains of Matabeleland north province. Modern high-rise offices counterpoint the mellow, graceful buildings of the colonial era.

Not yet a century old, the city's colourful history is so recent you feel you can almost reach out and touch it. And indeed you can lay your hand on the bark of the tree under which Lobengula held his indaba in the gardens of State House where Rhodes's rondavel still stands. Superbly-designed, magnificently-proportioned, the subsequent State House (formerly Government House) forms the impressive venue for the annual Independence Day celebrations held in Bulawayo.

The equally elegant City Hall complex, set in manicured lawns and pretty flower gardens, beautiful at night under floodlights, stands on the site of the 1896 laager where the first European population was

besieged. The well they sank for water can be seen in the gardens.

The tree where the first flag flew still blooms by the small building that was Dawson's Store — now part of a private hotel — which was run by James Dawson, trader and miner, who also served as an envoy for Lobengula.

And at the corner of Abercorn Street and Ninth Avenue, OK Bazaar occupies the spot where Rhodes's Bulawayo office stood. But the BSAC lion that once adorned the Rebellion Memorial, at the junction of Main Street and Selborne Avenue, was removed to Government House.

On one side of the City Hall stands the Bulawayo Art Gallery with its impressive collection of tapestries and paintings reflecting both western and African techniques.

The imposing headquarters of Zimbabwe National Railways overlooks the country's principal railway junction and marshalling yards — and the fascinating railway museum where Rhodes's private Pullman coach, a complete Victorian suite on wheels, befitting the grand, egocentric fancies of the man who allotted himself the task of empire builder, gives substance to the now fading shadows of that empire and his unfulfilled

Above: Members of Zion Christ Church, one of countless Christian sects that flourish in free Zimbabwe, at lively Sunday prayer meeting in Bulawayo.

Above: Weaver working handloom at Bulawayo's renowned Mzilikazi Craft Centre which produces a wide range of handmade craft products.

dreams. After his death in 1902, it carried his body from the Cape to Bulawayo.

Evidence enough of that ambition is contained in another exhibit: a proposal of 28 April, 1898, from Rhodes seeking British Government support to extend the railway another 800 miles to Lake Tanganyika.

Among other exhibits are the 1900 staff register, menus and table settings from the British Royal train of 1953, a letter of 28 May, 1897, from Rhodes appointing J. L. Bissett general manager of the Bechuanaland Railway at a salary of £1,200 a year, and old locomotives and rolling stock. One steam engine, *Jack Tar*, served the Mashonaland Railway Company Ltd. Another, number 257, made at the Falcon Engine and Car Works, Loughborough England in 1897, is a two-foot gauge loco that worked for many years on the Beira to Umtali (now Mutare) line before ending its life on a private forestry line in Zimbabwe.

Outside, in mint condition, are the coaches and locomotives of later eras — including one of the powerful 1929 Beyer Peacock steam giants designed by H. W. Garratt — and notices that evoke those days of old, such as one headed 'Prevention of Consumption' that earnestly exhorts

passengers 'to abstain from the dangerous and objectionable habit of expectorating'.

Rhodes's empirical ambition also sought to impose what he considered the 'civilizing' benefit of Christianity across Britain's sphere of influence in Africa and until 1962 a mobile mission constantly travelled the length and breadth of the railway network. The coach which carried the missionaries about their work — with its inscription, 'They brought light to the line' — is preserved inside the Museum.

Finally, a piece of twisted metal from a dynamite train that blew up on 15 June, 1940, leaving the landscape over several square kilometres in a state of devastation approaching that of a nuclear catastrophe, is a reminder of one of the region's grimmest tragedies.

Steam is perhaps the greatest legacy that the National Railways of Zimbabwe inherited at Independence. Its fleet of ninety-five steam locomotives were to have been phased out by the end of the 1970s but economic restraints, such as the high cost of spare parts for diesel locomotives, and Zimbabwe's plentiful supplies of coal, together with the skills available in the Bulawayo steam workshops, have ensured

Above: Tubers, cabbages, and tomatoes laid out for sale by enterprising street vendor in a Bulawayo suburb.

their continued viability.

Apart from taking much of the strain off the diesel and electric locomotive fleets, steam also stimulates tourism. Thousands of steam enthusiasts travel to Zimbabwe each year to admire and photograph its crack Class 15 Beyer Peacock locomotives and the NRZ draws more visitors with its special, and luxurious, steam safaris to places like Victoria Falls, when passengers relive the romantic days of old.

These safaris are operated by a private company in conjunction with the NRZ. The passengers, never more than twenty-four, travel in three specially restored coaches at the back of one of the mainline steam trains, complete with its own *cordon bleu* chef. The day starts with a champagne breakfast and there are overnight stops at national parks like Hwange where guests move from sleeping berth to luxurious hotel room. The company also runs a nine-day no-frills special simply for steam fanatics who want to travel all over Zimbabwe and ride footplate.

But it's not just steam that links past and present in Zimbabwe. Indeed, wherever you go, history constantly comes to life and confronts you — and both inside and outside the splendid museums found in almost every city and town, the country's relics and monuments are zealously maintained and guarded.

Bulawayo and its surrounding areas with their wealth of natural and manmade monuments and artefacts, some covering a span of thousands of years, are alive with history.

The city's rich heritage inspired the city's 1943 coat of arms with three hyrax — 'rock-rabbits' — courant and a crest composed of an African elephant 'with trunk elevated proper'. The city's Sindebele motto, 'Siye phambili' translates into 'We go forward'. The shield's red background signifies bloodshed. The hyrax are the totem of the Matabele royal family and symbolise the Matabele or Ndebele nation; the elephant, the emblem of Lobengula whose title among the Ndebele was *Ndhlovu*, meaning 'the elephant'.

The same heritage is also brought to vivid life in Bulawayo's outstanding Natural History Museum where the centrepiece is the second-largest mounted pachyderm in the world, known as the Doddieburn elephant. Standing more than eleven feet high at the shoulder, its two tusks weigh forty and forty-one kilos each. The exhibition hall which houses this is a stunning work of three-dimensional art. A family of guinea fowl struts through the undergrowth where a pride of mounted lions are poised on the bloody entrails of a wildebeest kill in the shade of plaster cast trees, to the recorded sounds of babbling streams and forest bird calls. Soft light bathes and brings to life the panoramic background painted in luminous pastel colours by artist Terry Donnelly.

The floor had to be specially reinforced to carry the weight of the Jumbo, but through half-closed eyes the atmosphere is charged with reality.

Imagination reflects itself in every hall of this magnificent museum; among the displays of African mammals and birds (including the 2,000-year-old fossil egg of an extinct Madagascar bird), in the gallery of an underground coal mine, through to the pony express coach built by Abbot, Downing Co., of Concord, New Hampshire, USA, which was

used by Royal Mail contractor C. H. Zeebenberg.

John Moffat, who quit the Inyati mission in 1865 and returned to Matabeleland in 1887 as British Representative to Lobengula's court, established the first mail service between Mafeking and Bulawayo a year later on 21 August, 1888. The first letters were postmarked 'Gubulawayo Bechuanaland' but for one day only. There are only thirteen extant copies of this postmark. Fearing it would offend Lobengula, the word Bechuanaland was removed from the stamp immediately.

Among the other exhibits in the museum are some from Robert Moffat's Inyati Mission, which still exists, and the gun carriage which bore Rhodes to his funeral in the Matobo Hills on 10 April, 1902.

The museum also houses all the flags that have fluttered over Rhodesia and Zimbabwe since his enterprise was first launched — one that endured from 1890 to 1923, and its successors — the flag that flew from 1923-52, the federation flag of 1953-63, the UDI flags of 1964-68 and 1968-79, the flag that flew briefly for six months in 1979 until 18 April, 1980, and finally the Zimbabwean flag that has flown throughout the country ever since.

Above: Paint gleaming, this old steam engine which was made in England in the last century, and worked the Mashonaland Railway Company's lines for many years, is now a star attraction in Bulawayo's Railway Museum.

Above: One of almost 100 steam locos still working on Zimbabwe National Railways hauls a load out of Bulawayo. Special steam safaris, in luxury coaches furbished as they were in the Victorian era, regularly ply out of Bulawayo to Victoria Falls.

Set in the beautiful grounds of Centenary Park, forty-five hectares of once arid land that were laid out and opened as a sylvan city retreat in 1953 to mark the centennial of the birth of Cecil John Rhodes, the museum is opposite Central Park which was developed to commemorate Bulawayo's city status on 4 November, 1943.

The fascinating variations of form, height, and colour of Central Park's magnificent fountain, built in the 1960s to celebrate the seventy-fifth anniversary of the founding of the city, are almost hypnotic, especially when the early morning light creates dazzling rainbows.

Both parks are renowned for the beauty of their tree-shaded, flower-filled gardens and walks along paths where banks of flowers and shrubs are broken by waterfalls. A large lake draws a rich variety of waterfowl and there's also an aviary. For children there's a miniature railway and a small fenced game park with some smaller wildlife species.

Bulawayo is all that a city of the twenty-first century should be, its handsome streets a riot of colour, especially when the jacaranda bloom between September and November, alive everywhere with the brilliant hues of bougainvillaea, aloes, and tropical and semi-tropical blooms.

Its citizens are ever close to nature. Five kilometres south of the city, Hillside Dam nature reserve and bird sanctuary makes a delightful picnic spot. And Tshabalala Wildlife Sanctuary, run by Zimbabwe's Department of National Parks and Wildlife Management, with giraffe, zebra and many antelope including tsesseby, impala, wildebeest, kudu, and many bird species, is only eight kilometres from the city centre on the road to the Matobo Hills.

For golf enthusiasts the city boasts three verdant, eighteen-hole courses — on Bulawayo Golf Course a memorial recalls the crash of The Silver Queen in March, 1920, which was written off just after takeoff on the last leg of the pioneer London to Cape flight (the flight was finished by a replacement plane).

As well as golf, there are several cricket and rugby grounds, tennis and squash courts, bowling greens, an Olympic-sized swimming pool in Central Park, and other sporting and recreational facilities including two first class football stadiums — not to forget the lush, green going of the Ascot racecourse where meetings are held twice a month. Horse racing, with a turnover of more than US$2.4 million a year, is a major industry employing several thousand people.

Though little used these days, Bulawayo also boasts an international motor racing circuit. But speedway, stock-car racing, cycle racing, athletics, boxing, and yachting regattas, are regular events on the city's sports calendar.

At the Mzilikazi Art and Craft centre new generations of artists, potters, sculptors, and other craftsmen are earning national and international recognition for the outstanding beauty of their work.

There's also a magnificent National Library and the permanent showground of Zimbabwe's annual International Trade Show with its landmark spire. With about 6,000 industries, the city is the nation's major economic force. For night life there are many fine restaurants, four cinemas, two drive-ins, two fine theatres, lively night clubs, and many discos.

First-class hotels include the upmarket, centrally-situated Bulawayo Sun and the splendidly comfortable Selborne Hotel, which in 1990 celebrated fifty years of traditional Anglo-Saxon inn-keeping in Africa. Nostalgia seeps out of every one of its timber beams, nowhere more so than in the King's Head, one of its five bars, with its chauvinistic but popular 'men only' ambience. No longer legally enforceable, the tradition is strictly maintained with shouts of 'stranger in the house' whenever a welcome, or unwelcome, woman enters.

Though it represented perhaps the pinnacle of all that he strove to achieve, Rhodes paid only a few visits to Bulawayo. But whenever he did he always made time to escape to Malindidzimu, the Ndebele's 'place of spirits', to sit on top of that great granite whaleback outcrop and contemplate the baroque grandeur that surrounds it.

No doubt, the Matobo's Malindidzimu matched the mood of his melancholic megalomania and his often ill-conceived and ill-fated attempts to extend the British Empire. Perhaps the immensity of this environment was something of an *alter ego* where he found the empathy which enabled him to renew his faith in himself and his vision.

Certainly Rhodes, who in his short lifetime wrote six wills and directed

Above: Sunk in solid granite, on the viewpoint he named 'World's View', Cecil John Rhodes' grave commands a vast panorama of the Matobo Hills.

Above: Westering sun reflects off the copper plaque on the grave of Dr. Leander Starr Jameson, Rhodes's right hand man in the British South Africa Company's imperial adventure, not far from the place where the body of his leader lies.

that when he died he should be set inside a grave scooped out of Malindidzimu's granite, had few if any doubts about his own greatness. The man whose last words on his deathbed are reported to have been 'so little done, so much to do' was confident enough that the world would remember him for the next 4,000 years for the inscription on the copper plate over his grave to read simply, 'Here lie the remains of Cecil John Rhodes'.

At least the frenzy that attended his last wishes justified his conceit, as did the immense, silent crowds that lined the streets of Bulawayo and who travelled with the cortege on the thirty-kilometre road specially built within days of his death, on 26 March, 1902, to carry him to his chosen grave.

Barely able to breathe during his last fortnight of life, Rhodes died at his Cape Town farm after a prolonged, debilitating, and painful illness. Vast crowds lined the Cape Town streets as his body was carried to the station and placed in his Pullman car for the train journey to Bulawayo where engineers led teams of navvies in a desperate race to complete the road to the foot of the Matobo Hills.

Similar crowds gathered in this city to pay homage to the empire builder before the final leg of the journey on 9 April when Rhodes's coffin was placed on a gun carriage. The route was long and arduous and the animals drawing the carriage rested overnight at his summer house.

The following day his coffin was lowered into the grave watched not only by a huge assembly of European mourners but by the disciplined ranks of the Ndebele chiefs and their warriors who escorted the cortege to Malindidzimu.

The planned last salute — a volley of rifles — was cancelled. The Ndebele feared that it would disturb the benign spirits of this place that Rhodes had named, 'View of the World'. Instead, as his coffin was lowered into its granite grave, fifteen kilometres from Mzilikazi's tomb at Ntumbane, the Ndebele spontaneously gave Rhodes the traditional salute normally accorded only to the Zulu kings — 'Bayete! Bayete! Bayete!'

There he lies, surrounded by massive rounded granite boulders that serve as guardian 'angels', overlooking a world in anguished confusion.

In his last will, Rhodes directed that Malindidzimu should be reserved as the burial ground of those who had done special service to Rhodesia and the British Empire. Subsequently his intimate Dr. Leander Starr Jameson, who served prison time for leading an 1895 raid against the Boers on Rhodes's instructions, was buried not far from Rhodes's grave.

Jameson died in London in 1917. But because of World War I his burial was delayed. The coffin did not leave England until early 1920 and he was buried in the Matobo in May. The inscription for this man who served as Prime Minister of the Cape between 1904-08, and became President of the BSAC in 1913, is even briefer than that on Rhodes's grave: 'Here lies Leander Starr Jameson'.

The third grave on Malindidzimu is that of Sir Charles Patrick John Coghlan, a lawyer who became the first Prime Minister of Rhodesia from 1923 until his death in 1927. He was interred three years later, on 14 August, 1930, some distance from the others, on the southern crest of the hill at a spot which was consecrated by Catholic rite.

Their simple, austere graves, with no headstones, counterpose the massive granite memorial which Rhodes raised before his death to Scottish-born Major Allan Wilson and the thirty-three men who went in pursuit of Lobengula after the king fled Bulawayo in November, 1893.

The patrol crossed the Shangani River and made contact with the Ndebele ruler. But rains had swollen the river. On 4 December, 1893, unable to return to Jameson's main force on the other bank, the patrol was surrounded by Lobengula's warriors and slaughtered.

They were buried where they fell but when Rhodes first saw Malindidzimu he decided at once to build there a memorial in their honour. Their bodies were reinterred in the Grecian-style mausoleum which has four bronze relief panels, by John Tweed, depicting their last stand. The names are all inscribed and the main dedication to the 'enduring memory of Allan Wilson and his men' states simply: 'There was no survivor.' There is also a memorial at the scene of the battle on the banks of the Shangani.

Now all is tranquil within these hills. The stronghold of the Ndebele warriors during the first *Chimurenga*, 'war of liberation', has become a

Above: Distinctive scriptural murals adorn the interior of the Cyrene Chapel in the Matobo Hills founded by the Reverend Edward Patterson. Encouraging African youngsters to develop their innate artistic talents, the Cyrene Mission has evolved into an internationally renowned school of art.

place of peace. Close to the centre of this 3,000-square-kilometre wilderness, 456 square kilometres, including Malindidzimu, make up Rhodes Matopos National Park.

The outliers of the Matobo are some thirty kilometres from Bulawayo. On the main route from Bulawayo, past Rhodes's old summer house, you come to the old Matobo rail terminus. The line was taken up in 1948. Ten kilometres from the rail terminus, along the gravel road to the right, is the Cyrene Mission, founded as an educational centre for African children in 1939, which has established its own art form, so distinctive that is known throughout the art world as the Cyrene School of Art.

The founding principal, the Reverend Edward Patterson, established its international renown. He encouraged his pupils to develop their innate artistic talents and highly individualistic African style. When he retired in 1953, the Cyrene interpretation of traditional scenes and religious depictions in colours and oils had become established as a unique art form. Though basically a secondary school, the Cyrene Mission continues to enhance its reputation as a complex and colourful school of art.

If you take the left turn to Rhodes Matopos National Park the road soon plunges into a strange and eerie world where, at every twist and turn, pantheons of granite gods, headless or caricatured deities, rise up in such profusion the mind is unable to assimilate them.

On one of the large granite whalebacks, Imadzi, is Njelele Cave with its famous rock paintings. It also has a shrine at its base dedicated to the men of the Memorable Order of Tin Hats — MOTH — who fell in the two World Wars. Nearby are the gates of Rowallan Park, set aside for the Girl Guide movement in memory of Baden-Powell who conceived the inspiration for the scouting movement in these dramatic hills.

These granites, the parent rocks of half Zimbabwe, were formed when molten masses deep beneath the earth thrust upwards. Among earth's oldest rocks, they cooled and solidified several hundred metres beneath the surface.

But during the course of three billion years, layers of soil and vegetation were stripped away by wind and rain through millennium upon millennium of weathering and erosion, leaving them exposed much as they were in their molten nascence.

It is such granite masses, split, seamed, sculpted, and shaped by time and weather, that form the whalebacks and castle kopjes that dominate 3,000 square kilometres of Matabeleland South Province.

Forty thousand years ago, the caves and crevices formed out of the rocks became home to Zimbabwe's earliest inhabitants, the 'San'. Twenty thousand years or so later, San artists began painting on the walls of the caves and cliff faces, using pigments and natural minerals that have survived the vagaries of climate and time.

These paintings are found all over Zimbabwe, wherever there are granite outcrops, and although more than 2,000 sites have been identified and catalogued, experts believe that many more priceless Stone Age art treasures have yet to be discovered, particularly within these awesome hills.

The processes of cooling affected the granite in many different ways: some split in regular vertical and horizontal patterns, and water and

weather enlarged these cracks. As a result, many became a series of great boulders, balanced one on top of the other.

In other instances, upright sheets of granite simply fell away leaving a fresh, clean vertical face — an ideal 'canvas' for these early artists. Another process turned some into large, shallow caves whose smooth concave and convex walls and ceilings provided the San painters with their greatest opportunity.

Such caves are the richest repository of this, the earliest of art forms. Almost inevitably the views from these caves, high above the ground, were panoramic, some stretching for at least 100 kilometres, and provided a great deal of artistic inspiration.

Many paintings, using earth pigments like ochre, in reds, browns, and yellows, are at levels well out of standing reach. None of the paintings have been dated effectively but experts agree that they belong to the Late Stone Age, and date from somewhere between the last 30,000 and 1,000 years. At least one has been dated to 8,500 years ago.

The most recent works incorporate all the different media used before: polychrome figures, landscapes, complicated cryptographs, and finally

Above: Immaculate baked earth houses and compound of a Ndebele homestead in the arid, unproductive Khumalo Communal Lands at Silozwane, not far from Bulawayo.

black and white or plastered kaolin works. When the clay fell off, etched in white among the black lichens were impressive and dramatic works of art.

What is certain is that the eight major sites in the Matobo represent all that is best in this highly-stylised and unique art form, bound up with the life of prehistoric man — his hunting, dances, and spiritual beliefs. Of these, those in a cave at Silozwane in Khumalo Communal Land, and the White Rhino Shelter, are considered among the most outstanding.

The drive to Silozwane takes you along a winding, dusty road through the tribal trustlands and villages of mud and thatch houses, each one decorated with colourful designs painted on the exterior walls with earth pigments, much as the first San painters did their work.

Finally, you arrive at the foot of a massive whaleback to follow painted arrows up a precipitous 300-foot trail and an airy scramble across the exposed lower face of the domed hill to a huge cave; not for those who suffer vertigo.

The back wall of the cave served as an enormous canvas. The centrepiece is a six-foot-high etching of a giraffe and an even larger antelope-headed snake. Other animals depicted on the wall are lion, rhinoceros, kudu, tsesseby, impala, zebra, elephant, birds in flight, hunters armed with bows and arrows; and an incredibly-detailed flying termite. Even the veins in its wings are shown.

Similar images are grafted on to the wall of the White Rhino Shelter, with remarkable delicacy considering the coarse surface. A line of dark red hunters is superimposed over a herd of wildebeest and there are caricatures of people with a small flock of guinea fowl in the lower panel.

These caves, with their mystical atmosphere, profoundly influenced the communities that made their home in and around these hills. Within the last 1,000 years the Mbire Shoko community, a Bantu Shona group, migrated south from East Africa's Lake Tanganyika bringing with them their monotheistic belief in one supreme creator. Their faith found its greatest expression in Great Zimbabwe, where it became the centralizing religious authority, and in the Matobo Hills. The caves which inspired the San artists became the spiritual shrines of the Mbire, known as the *Mwari*.

During the fifteenth century, at the height of the Rozvi Empire which was finally overthrown by Mzilikazi, the Shona frequently visited these shrines each of which had an oracle, the voice of the Mwari. So powerful was this faith that it spread across the Limpopo and was taken up by the Vendao community.

This spirituality attained its greatest strength in the Matobo. Indeed, it eventually became known as *Mwari ve-Matojeni*, God of the Matopos. It was adopted by the Ndebele whose reverence for the Matobo is sacred. They called the creator *Mulimu*, provider of rain, guardian of nature, and sought divine intercession whenever calamity threatened. It was after consultation with the priests, priestesses, and oracles of the place of the benevolent spirits that the Ndebele took up arms against the Europeans in 1896.

Early Christian missionaries like the Moffat family recognised the purity of the Shona and Ndebele belief in the unknowable High God, the one creator, and adopted the local concept into their scriptural teachings,

Above: Silozwane Cave, atop a massive granite whaleback in the outliers of the Matobo Hills, where some of the most outstanding examples of 'San' rock art have survived for thousands of years.

thus making it synonymous with the Christian faith.

Mwari shrines are still held in reverential awe by local communities and ceremonies to appease the ancestral spirits, overcome ill-fortune, and particularly to make rain, are still held in the Matobo Hills, and at other sacred places throughout Zimbabwe.

Those visiting these hills for the first time will not be surprised that they are a bastion of invincible faith. Described, rightly, as among the most majestic granite scenery on earth, they emanate an overwhelming sense of power, a power far greater than that of mankind. They certainly affected Rhodes profoundly. Undoubtedly he sensed in their majesty an even greater will than he could ever hope to exert — they were perhaps the one place where even he felt a sense of humility.

But the impression of an alien world is softened by its beauty. Despite its gaunt and rocky profile, none of this land is barren. Among the trees that have taken root on the most unlikely ledges, and in the floors of the many valleys, are mountain acacia and vividly-coloured msasas and blood-red erythrinas while many ground orchids and flowering plants carpet the grasslands with pastel colours.

The hills are cut by diamond-bright streams and waterfalls some of which have been dammed to form small lakes and reservoirs; the sanctity implicit in their nature finding expression as a geological, botanical, and wildlife wonderland.

Set in a group of rocks near the entrance to the Matobo Hills game park is the grave of Lobengula's sister, Nini, who was executed on his orders for her illicit affair with a commoner. The king loved his sister deeply but was forced by public outrage to condemn her. She asked

Right: 'San' — Bushman — hunter depicted on a rock painting at Silozwane Cave.

her executioners to strangle her with her own girdle.

Inside the game park, endangered but docile white rhino pause as they forage in the grasslands by the roadside against the unique backdrop of the hills. Stately sable, graceful impala, agile klipspringer, an antelope of the rocks and cliffs, wildebeest, the 'clown of the plains', zebra, buffalo, giraffe, leopard, baboon, vervet monkey, squirrels, and the rock hyrax (known as the 'dassie' or rock-rabbit) are also found in abundance within these hills and valleys.

Guinea fowl quarter the ground constantly in idle search for pickings while eagles and other raptors soar on the constant daytime thermals looking for carrion.

On the winding road to Maleme Dam, temples of doom, towers of stone, surrealistic images of Buddha, grinning gargoyles, giant dwarfs, reptilian monsters, rock pyramids, and sublime sphinxes flash by in an endless blur.

The notice at the dam prohibits swimming and warns, 'Beware of bilharzia, crocs, and humps'. It goes unheeded. In this bizarre landscape caution is a banal consideration.

On the lake shores comfortable thatched lodges and caravan and camping sites run by the national parks allow visitors to enjoy the magnificent beauty of these surroundings where a silver paper moon, pasted on an ice-blue sky, rises in the cleft of a cliff washed in orange by the sun's dying rays, and bream, barbel, and black bass chasing midges break the still surface of the water.

In such a place at such a time, *Mwari*, the supreme creator, seems supremely close.

The Maleme Wilderness Area forms a salient alongside the road south-west to the village of Kezi, some ninety-six kilometres from Bulawayo, which serves as a trading centre for the large cattle ranches in the area. This land was once rich in wildlife and fourteen kilometres outside the village, along a dirt trail, is Antelope Mine, where hundreds of years ago gold was mined.

The workings of the ancients were discovered in 1890 and the first claim pegged in 1894. The wildlife gave the mine its name but actual mining did not begin until 1913, and after five years the mine was closed down never to reopen. Some thirty kilometres beyond the old mine the trading centre of Legion Mine takes its name from another abandoned gold mine.

East of Antelope Mine is the Tuli-Makwe Dam, built in 1966 on the Tuli river which rises in the Matobo Hills and flows south to join Botswana's Shashi River.

At the border it passes through the spot where Selous established a hunting base and the BSAC's mercenary Pioneer Column built its first fort in 1890. For three years it was the main point of entry from South

Above: Midday sun and shadow highlight the chevron wall of the Natalale Ruins, considered the most magnificent ancient stone wall in southern Africa.

Africa but when the route through Beitbridge was opened Tuli ceased to be of any importance. Today all that marks the place where the fort stood is the flag that flutters over the Pioneer Memorial.

Beitbridge, the main border post with South Africa just over 100 kilometres from Fort Tuli, is marked by the kilometre and a half span of the road-rail bridge across the Limpopo.

It was built between 1927 and 1929 with money from the Beit Trust, a £1.2 million fund established as a bequest of Alfred Beit, Cecil Rhodes's closest associate, who died in 1906. Other bridges it financed during the 1920s-30s were the Otto Beit Bridge and the Birchenough Bridge. The Beit Trust Gallery, a collection of valuable art works including many of Thomas Baines's paintings, is in the care of the National Archives.

Two roads lead out of Beitbridge; one north-east to Masvingo, the other north-west, back to Bulawayo through West Nicholson, once a copper and asbestos mining centre but now a major cattle ranching headquarters, and the town of Colleen Bawn, an odd name to find on a map of Africa.

It rose up around a gold claim staked by an Irish prospector in 1895 who named it after the sweetheart he left behind in Dublin. Romantic he might have been, but wealth he did not find. Today Colleen Bawn is noted for its unromantic cement industry.

Not far beyond is the mining centre of Gwanda and then Mbalabala, close to the Umzingwane Dam, built in 1958 and now a watersports centre for Bulawayo citizens. Halfway between Mbalabala and Bulawayo is the tungsten and gold mining centre of Esigodini, which once rejoiced in the nostalgic name of Essexvale, no doubt the result of a bout of home sickness in one of the early prospectors.

Nineteen kilometres on from Esigodini is Chipingali Wildlife Orphanage, a haven for sick, and unwanted animals and birds founded in 1973 by Viv Wilson, former Director of Bulawayo Natural History Museum. Now run by a Trust, it is also the centre of a major duiker conservation project.

Many of the orphanage's animals — either through disability or because they were reared from birth as pets — will never leave this sanctuary. Some of the birds in the handsome aviary have lost wings or legs and left to fend for themselves would simply die.

But whenever possible Chipingali's lame and laggard are rehabilitated to the wild. Its greatest success story so far is that of a troop of vervet monkeys. Led by a former house pet, this was settled on an island in Lake Kariba where its numbers have flourished and multiplied. The orphanage is entirely dependent on public donations and sponsorship.

Plumtree, a ranching centre 100 kilometres west of Bulawayo, is the border post between Zimbabwe and Botswana. Intending visitors to Matabeleland used to pass this way a century and a half ago.

Thirty-two kilometres to the west of the main road is Mangwe Pass with its memorial to Moffat and his fellow missionaries who travelled along this route in 1854. It is also the site of a fort built by the Pioneer Column in their attempt to conquer Matabeleland and a place known as Lee's house, built by an ex-Royal Naval officer, John Lee. A confidant of Mzilikazi, he was a loyal friend. After he refused to

Above: An unmistakable bird of prey, the Augur Buzzard inevitably chooses a well-placed perch from which to scout out its victim.

cooperate with the BSAC during the 1893 suppression of the Ndebele his house and 500 square kilometres of land given to him by Mzilikazi were confiscated.

Sixty kilometres or so further along the Plumtree-Bulawayo road the borders of Mzilikazi's territory were marked by a large fig tree where visitors waited for royal permission to enter the kingdom. The custom is commemorated today by the village, called Figtree, that now stands there.

But perhaps the most important historic site along this route, seventeen kilometres beyond Figtree, is the imposing fifteenth-, or sixteenth-century ruins of Khami, the old capital of the Torwa State, the second-largest known stone ruins in Zimbabwe, dating from around the same time as Great Zimbabwe.

Spread over hundreds of hectares, the ruins — where the Rozvi's Mambo dynasty held court — later became an important spiritual shrine for the Ndebele and were closely-guarded by Lobengula. Indeed, before 1893 Europeans knew only of them by word of mouth and the earliest maps of the area mark them as 'The King's Preserve'.

Evidence of 40,000 years of continuous occupation has been uncovered. Khami flourished until the 1830s when the Zulu's Nguni warriors, retreating from Mzilikazi's advance, destroyed it.

Later, Lobengula and his *induna* used it for the Ndebele's sacred rainmaking ceremonies. No doubt, they acquired some of the ritual for these from the Shona for whom rainmaking is one of the most important ceremonies.

The Shona still practice these rainmaking rites in their sacred shrines, every year between September and January, with petitions to the tribe's ancestral spirits. All are involved — providing music, food, drink, and dancers. Honey and millet beer is an essential ingredient and the songs and dances an appeasement of the spirits that control the clouds.

Zimbabwe's rainfall is often erratic and in 1971 the country's meteorologists introduced another form of rainmaking ceremony which also takes place each year between November and March. Planes are deployed to measure the raindrop spectrum of the cumulus clouds and, where necessary, seed them with silver iodide crystals. On some occasions this technique has yielded as much as 120 tonnes of rain for each cloud so treated.

The first investigation of the Khami Ruins was disastrous. It was carried out by the Rhodesia Ancient Ruins Company which had a franchise to explore old gold mines and other places for treasure. As at Great Zimbabwe, and other archaeological sites, they did untold damage and found precious little in the way of gold or treasure — only the priceless relics that the searchers destroyed thinking they were worthless.

It was not until 1947 that the first serious excavations and studies were undertaken at Khami by K. R. Robinson, the Chief Inspector of Historical Monuments, when late Stone Age artefacts were uncovered.

Khami's central complex is made up of twelve ruins. On the Hill Ruin many of the hut floors are still visible and the charred timbers of the passageways tell of a terrible conflagration.

A cross in one of the ruins is an enigma: some postulate that it was

Above: Klipspringer stands guard on a rock outcrop. Known as the chamois of Africa, the hooves of these denizens of cliffs and mountain slopes are specially adapted to their stony and precipitous environment — and their thick coat cushions the shock of falls.

Above: Christian cross, believed to have been laid by Portuguese missionaries in the seventeenth or eighteenth centuries at the Khami Ruins, seat of secret rituals performed by the Ndebele to appease the spirits. Khami was destroyed in the early nineteenth century by the Zulu Nguni warrior clan when they fled from Mzilikazi.

left behind by Portuguese missionaries who may have visited the capital in the seventeenth or eighteenth centuries. But many of the implements found on the site, now contained in the nearby museum, are more than 1,000 years old. Much has yet to be learned from these ancient stones — and from other ancient ruins close to Bulawayo.

The first of these lies to the east beyond Heaney Junction — named after a member of the Pioneer Column — close to Fort Rixon. South-east of this once stockaded village, where the first white settlers entrenched themselves against the marauding Ndebele in 1896, stand the Regina Ruins. Comprising an old fortification made up of a series of six large terraces built around a granite kopje, they also suffered much damage in the 1890s from the Ancient Ruins Company and other treasure seekers. On the way you pass 'Cumming's Store', scene of a fierce 1896 battle and the grave of Sergeant J. O'Leary who was killed by the Ndebele. Close by the Regina Ruins, to the north, are the Danagombe Ruins — still known as the Dhlo-Dhlo — which are contemporaneous to the Khami Ruins and where the ruling Mambo held Portuguese visitors and missionaries captive. Excavations have uncovered their religious icons.

And twenty-six kilometres from these ruins stands a high, mound-shaped kopje with what is undoubtedly the most magnificent ancient stone wall in southern Africa. But before its builders could finish their fortifications they were overwhelmed by Swazi *impis* raiding far from the south. The beauty of the Natalale ruins is in the intricate herring-bone, chevron, chequer patterns of stones of contrasting colour woven into the main wall.

Not far from here, close to the Shangani River bridge, also stands the Pongo Memorial, erected to the memory of those who died in the Pongo Reserve during the 1896 rebellion.

It was on the banks of this river that Lobengula's envoy, Dawson, who volunteered to lead the search, found the bodies of Allan Wilson and his men, slaughtered in the battle with Lobengula's warriors. He buried them there, near an ant hill, and on the large mopane tree which shaded their grave carved the words: 'To Brave Men'. The trunk of that tree has since been taken to Bulawayo's National Museum.

Wherever you go in this region history is not only recorded, but also preserved. Indeed, eighty kilometres north of Bulawayo on the road to Eastnor, past long abandoned gold workings like Turk Mine, stands Moffat's 130-year-old Inyati Mission.

Some distance beyond this is Lonely Mine, once the deepest quartz reef mine in Africa. Now, although gold is still mined, the copper mine opened by Lonrho in the 1960s is the lodestone of the region's wealth.

Stretching more than 500 kilometres across the centre of Zimbabwe, north-east from Guruve to Mberengwa in the south-west, runs a ridge of 200-million-year-old hills ranging in width from three to eleven kilometres. This is Zimbabwe's treasury, a fabulously rich repository of all the fabled metals of legendary Ophir.

Few nations in the world possess the mineral wealth that lies in the seams and veins that run all through the Great Dyke and in the plateaux that stretch away on either side.

Buried deep in the Plutonic rocks of its upper layers are gold and silver, platinum and tungsten, copper and chrome, iron and tin, magnesite and asbestos, emeralds and diamonds.

For hundreds of years, from at least the seventh century AD, alluvial gold has been recovered from the sediment of rivers and streams. And as far back as the twelfth century people dug primitive mines to recover the precious metal. Just under 100 years ago, many of these ancient mines were pegged and claimed by the European prospectors who flocked to this new Eldorado.

Some were soon exhausted. But gold remains one of Zimbabwe's largest sources of foreign currency, overshadowed only by tobacco, bringing more than US$115 million a year in the late 1980s against the US$155 million earned from the combined extraction of asbestos, nickel, coal, copper, chrome and iron. In 1990, a joint Zimbabwe-Australian project began mining the country's rich lodes of platinum.

A geological mosaic, these minerals from the deep interior of the earth created intrusions in the country's ancient granitic strata and were the central factor in the country's early economy. Gold was bartered for goods and exported to Asia and Europe through such Indian Ocean ports as Sofala, controlled by the Arabs and, later, the Portuguese. Iron too was exploited but the mining and smelting processes were equally primitive.

Modern technology, both in mining and smelting and refining, has made today's mineral extraction much more sophisticated and diverse with the production of more than forty minerals and metals, accounting for almost half the country's exports and seven per cent of the GDP.

The great majority of this mineral wealth, especially gold, lies in or alongside the Great Dyke. Throughout the well-developed farmlands, large-scale mining and processing operations have transformed the Zimbabwe Midlands — from Gweru to Harare and beyond — into the nation's industrial heartland. Indeed, so important is this area to the national economic well-being that the railway line between the capital and Gweru was the first to be electrified — in 1983.

But although this intensive industrial activity, particularly smelting, refining, and steelmaking, has left some deep and permanent scars across the land, they are scarcely seen. Apart from an occasional intrusive cooling tower or giant chimney-stack, industrial development remains hidden from the passing eye and there is little of the squalor and pollution found in the industrialised nations of the north.

Indeed, wherever you travel in Zimbabwe's industrial Midlands, cattle ranches and arable farms turn a fresh and verdant face to the African sun. Here among the ranches and farms, mines and steelworks, are wildlife sanctuaries, lakes, forested hills, and scenic waterfalls. All the

Above: Floral tribute at Heroes' Acre, where those who died that Zimbabwe might be freed from minority rule lie in honour.

Previous pages: Harare City Centre. In distant background stands the kopje where the Pioneer Column made camp in September 1890, signalling Rhodes's annexation of the land that was to become Zimbabwe.

Above: Interior of Zimbabwe's national Military Museum, Gweru.

Midlands cities are adorned with handsome, tree-lined avenues, and flower-filled parks and gardens.

Indeed, where else in the world can a day's organised sightseeing (as at Kwekwe) include a visit to a gold mine, gold processing plant, steelworks, mayor's parlour — and a nature walk in a wildlife park among eland, zebra, wildebeest, sable, kudu, tsesseby, impala, and wart hog, bird sanctuary, and botanical gardens? Where man's industry dominates the horizon, Zimbabwe still cherishes its natural marvels.

For most, the country's industrial belt starts 164 kilometres north-east of Bulawayo at Gweru, the country's third-largest city with more than 200,000 people. Lying 277 kilometres south-west of Harare, it was founded in 1894 by Dr. Jameson as a coaching station on the Harare-Bulawayo road. Within the year there were six hotels and it had become a settlement for gold prospectors combing the seams of the Great Dyke.

Its first bank opened in 1896, followed two years later by the Stock Exchange which still stands in the town centre. One of the country's pioneer newspapers, the *Northern Optimist*, now the *Gweru Times*, was launched in 1897.

The arrival of the railway — from both the north and the south — in 1902, however, was the catalyst which triggered Gweru's development. Then called Gwelo — the name was changed in 1982 — it was elevated to municipal status in 1914 and became a city in 1971.

Its wide streets, with their graceful buildings, attractively laid out among green lawns, colourful flowerbeds, and stands of tall and shady trees, come as revelation to those preconceived images conjured by its reputation as the industrial centre of the country.

In fact, until the end of the 1930s it was mainly a farming centre, serving the many arable, cattle, and dairy farms that flourish in the region. The pleasant city centre, dominated by Boggie's Clock Tower, with the Midlands Hotel on one side and the old Stock Exchange building on the other, still retains its farming ambience.

The clock, with the hands standing at 10.50, and tower were raised in memory of Major W. J. Boggie, born in Scotland in 1865, by his widow Mrs Jeannie Boggie in 1937, nine years after his death. Town legend says that his remains were interred in the tower and that when, one day in 1981, they were removed at 10.50 the clock stopped — never to move again.

The elegance of Gweru's early colonial architecture is perhaps best seen in the old 1905 magistrate's court in Lobengula Avenue, now a government administrative office. From a more recent era, the city's splendid municipal offices, in graceful curved profile, are set in a delightful rose garden containing a stone from Waterloo Bridge, presented to the city fathers by London County Council. Close by, in a secluded avenue stands another antiquity, more of interest for what it represents than for its design. Gweru's Dutch Reform Church, a branch of the South African faith that espoused and spread the gospel of apartheid, still serves worshippers, tangible proof of the country's

Above: Eland in stunted scrub woodlands near the Zimbabwe capital of Harare. Largest of all antelopes, eland weigh almost a ton but can leap more than two metres (seven feet) from a standing position.

Above: Locals fishing in a reservoir near Harare, capital of Zimbabwe.

commitment to freedom of worship.

Of the city's two public swimming pools, the Memorial Swimming Baths, behind the magnificent auditorium in the Civic Centre with its carved wooden mural depicting theatre through the ages, were built as a 1920 memorial to those citizens who fell in the Great War. There are cinemas, a comfortable and comprehensive library, music academy, and almost eighty members' clubs. And, nine kilometres from the town, Antelope Game Park with forty-five kilometres of game-viewing roads has abundant wildlife including, in particular, sable and giraffe.

In the more densely settled residential areas of the western suburbs, subsidised housing and schools, play centres, clinics, swimming pools, libraries, and sports centres ensure a full and satisfying quality of life even for low-income workers and their families. In the more open, less settled suburbs there is an eighteen-hole championship golf course, and gliding, sailing, riding, and motor racing clubs.

Gweru is an important army and air force training centre and it is appropriate that the outstanding Midlands Museum should serve as the country's National Army and Aviation Museum. The weapons hall and the displays outside of different generations of aircraft and ground armour — tanks, personnel carriers, field guns — are striking visual exhibitions.

Among the biplanes and early jet fighters is the strange-looking 'le-pou-du-cielf' — Flying Flea — built by Aston Redrup of Bulawayo in 1933 from a design by Henri Mignet, powered by a 540 cc two-stroke motorcycle engine. With a top speed of 100 kilometres an hour, this odd plane needed less than 100 metres for take off and landed at a speed of thirty kilometres an hour. It had an endurance of three hours and a ceiling of 5,000 feet.

The most interesting historical exhibition, however, is contained in the

Left: Tobacco burgeons in the fertile soils of the Midlands. Zimbabwe's major export crop brings the world's second largest producer annual foreign exchange of more than US$150 million.

Military History gallery. Attractive graphics detail the wars of freedom fought in Zimbabwe during the last 1,000 years, ending with a display that salutes the martyrs and heroes of the most recent liberation struggle. The first large-scale industry to establish itself in Gweru was the multinational shoe manufacturer, Bata, which opened its manufacturing plant in 1939. Now the largest in Southern Africa, it produces more than ten million pairs of shoes a year for both the local and export market. In the years since, following in the company's footsteps, so to speak, many more large industries have established manufacturing units at Gweru.

Roughly at the heart of the country, Gweru is the central axis of the vast Southern African rail network where main lines from Maputo and Johannesburg join the Bulawayo-Gweru-Harare trunk line which, from Harare, also serves the line to Beira and, from Bulawayo, the line to Zambia.

The large marshalling yard in the city's Dabuka suburb — sixty kilometres of track covering several square kilometres — includes the country's largest container terminal. There's another large marshalling yard at Somabhula, twenty-seven kilometres south-west of Gweru, which is the physical junction of the Maputo and Johannesburg lines.

The junction takes its name from a famous African elephant hunter of old, Shamaburu, who lived in the area. It became a boom town in 1903 when a European prospector, R. H. Mois, discovered diamonds in the local forest, as well as sapphire and chrysoberyl but these deposits were too small to be commercially viable.

To the east, between Somabhula and Shurugwi, is one of Gweru's major resort centres, the sylvan shores of Gwendoro Lake, formed by the dam built on the Runde River in 1958 to create a major reservoir for Gweru's water needs. The five-square-kilometre lake that formed behind the dam is now a boating and fishing resort.

And thirty-five kilometres to the south, their highest point rising 5,000 feet above sea level, the chrome-rich Shurugwi hills of Zimbabwe's Great Dyke form another wooded weekend resort for Gweru citizens.

Despite the nearby mine workings, Shurugwi was a noted beauty spot for many decades but late in 1989, shrouded in mist, the doors and windows of its massive Grand Hotel barred and shuttered, the 'For Sale' signs long faded, the town — birthplace of Sir Roy Welensky, first prime minister of the Federation of Rhodesia and Nyasaland — seemed to have returned to the limbo of its long ago past, nestling in a tree-shrouded valley, a pleasant but forgotten mining backwater despite the modern scenic highway that winds south over the forested hills to the sweltering plains below.

Founded in the 1890s as Sebanga Poort, at the seat of one of the world's largest chrome deposits, it changed its name to Selukwe in January, 1896, and became Shurugwi after Independence. The name comes from the Ndebele word for pig pen.

Years ago Ferny Creek, a small valley beyond the town's immaculate golf course, was a well-developed day resort with rest huts, camping site, caravan park, many picnic spots, and swimming pool. But now the trail is overgrown and the swimming pool empty save for the rainwater that fills the bottom of the deep end.

Apart from chrome, Shurugwi was once rich in gold. In less than two

Above: Ancient bushman rock paintings preserved on the shores of Lake McIlwaine Recreational Park.

decades, one mine alone produced more than 300,000 fine ounces from more than two million tonnes of ore.

Shurugwi's first banker, Alfred Ellenberger, once helped to rescue one gold mine from liquidation — not as a financial expert but as a diviner. When the head of the Glen Rosa mine told him it would have to close down because it did not have enough gold to justify continuing, Ellenberger offered his divining services.

Inspecting the mine workings with his divining rod, the bank manager told the mine manager that all he had to do was dig down another two metres to find gold. Within days, more than $8,000 in gold had been recovered — a considerable sum in the second decade of the century — and the Glen Rosa mine prospered for many years.

Now the gold mines are abandoned but chrome continues to contribute to this sleepy hill capital's prosperity. The mines are worked by the giant multinational Union Carbide.

On the scenic drive south, over Wolfshall Pass, hidden deep in the valley beside the road are the beautiful Dunraven and Camperdown Falls, found by following a steep downhill path through the forest.

Another delightful resort for city dwellers lies an equal distance to the east of Gweru — Whitewaters Dam, built on the Kwekwe River in 1948 to form the first of Gweru's major reservoirs. The road from Gweru to White Waters follows roughly the alignment of the Masvingo branch railway line, through Lalapansi, a small farming and mining centre, to Mvuma, a once prosperous gold town, where the road joins the Harare-Masvingo Road.

You know you are approaching the town by the landmark chimney stack of the old Falcon Gold and Copper Mine which is visible for many kilometres around. Gold was first discovered here in 1903 but it was another eleven years before mining began. It became a boom town.

Above: Muslim mosque in the industrial town of Kwekwe at the heart of the Zimbabwe midlands.

For at least a decade, the Falcon mine produced more gold and copper than any other in the country but then the seams ran out and in 1925 the mine was closed. Now this small town slumbers on, undisturbed by dreams of wealth, content with its place in Zimbabwe's gold rush history.

From Mvumu, the road to Harare runs through pleasant farmlands and the old Afrikaner town of Chivhu, then Featherstone, and the gold mining town of Beatrice — named after the sister of Pioneer Corps officer Henry Borrow — past McIlwaine Recreational Park to Harare.

In a straight line westwards, about halfway between Mvuma and Kwekwe, is Sebakwe, another recreational park renowned for its beautiful surroundings. Formed when the Sebakwe River was dammed in 1957, it was closed in 1982 for some time while the dam wall was raised another twenty-three feet, substantially increasing the surface area of the lake.

The main attraction of this small, twenty-seven-square-kilometre recreation park, which is open all year round, is its coarse fishing. Nature walks through wildlife areas are also popular. The park is fifty-four kilometres south of Kwekwe and there are overnight cottages, camping, and caravan sites.

Astonishingly, though Kwekwe and its twin, the steel town of Redcliff, also describe themselves as the industrial heart of Zimbabwe, even this town is the centre of a substantial wildlife hunting and photographic safari industry. Indeed, here where rhino roam the countryside within sight of belching chimney stacks and opencast workings, predators like leopard stalk antelope.

But for all that, Kwekwe's genesis and continued existence are based in the excoriating fires of its steel furnaces and thermal power stations. With its wide boulevards, lined by immaculate lawns and flowering

Above: Prefabricated paper house at Kwekwe's Globe and Phoenix gold mine, imported in 1895 as the manager's residence, has survived almost a century. Now the National Museum of Gold Mining, the papier mache outer panels are reinforced by wire. The inner panels are made of cardboard.

trees, smart town centre and the elegant Cape-style architecture of its post office, Kwekwe would pass anywhere else in the world for a genteel country market town. Originally called Sebakwe, the town, which began its life as a BSAC fort, changed its name to Kwekwe, derived from the croaking sound of the frogs in the Kwekwe river, in 1905.

Rich in both minerals and farmlands, major crops likes maize, soya beans, sorghum, cotton, coffee and citrus fruits make this region one of the granaries of Zimbabwe and an important centre for cash crops. In fact, Kwekwe's farmers produce ten per cent of the winter cereals grown in Zimbabwe. There are also extensive cattle ranches and dairy farms.

The National Breweries — Natbrew — located their maltings plant in Kwekwe because of the high quality barley grown in the region. Producing more than 21,000 tonnes of malt a year, some fifty per cent of this is exported to neighbouring African countries.

The most fascinating part of a visit to Kwekwe is the National Museum devoted to gold mining — and the parastatal roasting plant for the gold industry which processes around 500 kilos of gold a year for eight gold mines in the region on a 'no profit, no loss' basis. It also refines silver.

The museum, next to the head offices of the Globe and Phoenix Mine, is located in one of Africa's most unusual buildings — a prefabricated paper house built in 1894. The papier mache outer panels are reinforced with wire, the inner panels are cardboard. These are mounted on a wooden framework.

Three of these buildings were imported into Zimbabwe in the last decade of the last century. The other two — at Bulawayo and Harare, then Salisbury — no longer exist. The paper house at Kwekwe was the residence of the mine's general manager for about two years and was then turned into offices and finally used as a store room.

The creosote-treated wooden piles on which it was built have ensured its continued existence. Next to it is a thatched rondavel built of corrugated iron. Because of their historical significance, it is these two buildings which house the National Museum of Gold Mining.

Specimens of gold-bearing quartz rock are on display as well as a working model of a gold mine, complete with ore-crushing machinery. Outside are many other machines used in the processing of gold.

After almost a century of continuous production, the Globe and Phoenix Mine, once one of the country's richest mines, ceased mining operations in 1988 with the loss of more than 1,000 jobs. But in 1989 work was going ahead on a short-term project of between three and five years to recover gold from the waste ore that has piled up over the last ninety years.

The nearby Zimbabwe mining and smelting plant, one of the largest in the world, produces more than 150,000 tonnes of high grade carbon ferrochrome a year.

Kwekwe is approximately halfway — 220 kilometres — between Bulawayo and Harare. Its twin, the steel city of Redcliff, lies fourteen kilometres to the south. Neat housing estates, town centre, and the offices of Zisco, the steel company, stand on one side of a pleasant, tree-clad hill, iron workings and steelmaking plant — close to a seemingly bottomless hole in the ground — on the other.

Redcliff prospers because of Zimbabwe's unusually large deposits of iron ore and limestone and the abundance of coal available from Hwange collieries. The plant is capable of producing a million tonnes of liquid steel a year.

Sixty kilometres west of Kwekwe along a dirt road is Silobela, the main trading centre for the small-scale peasant farmers in the Silobela Communal Lands. There is also a limited amount of gold mining. Another dirt road leads north-west from Kwekwe to the edge of the Mafungabusi Plateau and the remote settlement of Gokwe at the heart of the forested Gokwe Communal Lands where peasants tend their smallholdings far from the hectic pace and bustle of twentieth-century Zimbabwe.

To the north, thirty-two kilometres beyond Kwekwe, Umnyati is the location of one of Zimbabwe's first thermal power stations, built in 1938 and considerably enlarged in 1974. Roughly the same distance beyond that is the road west to the Empress and Commoner mines, one producing gold, the other copper.

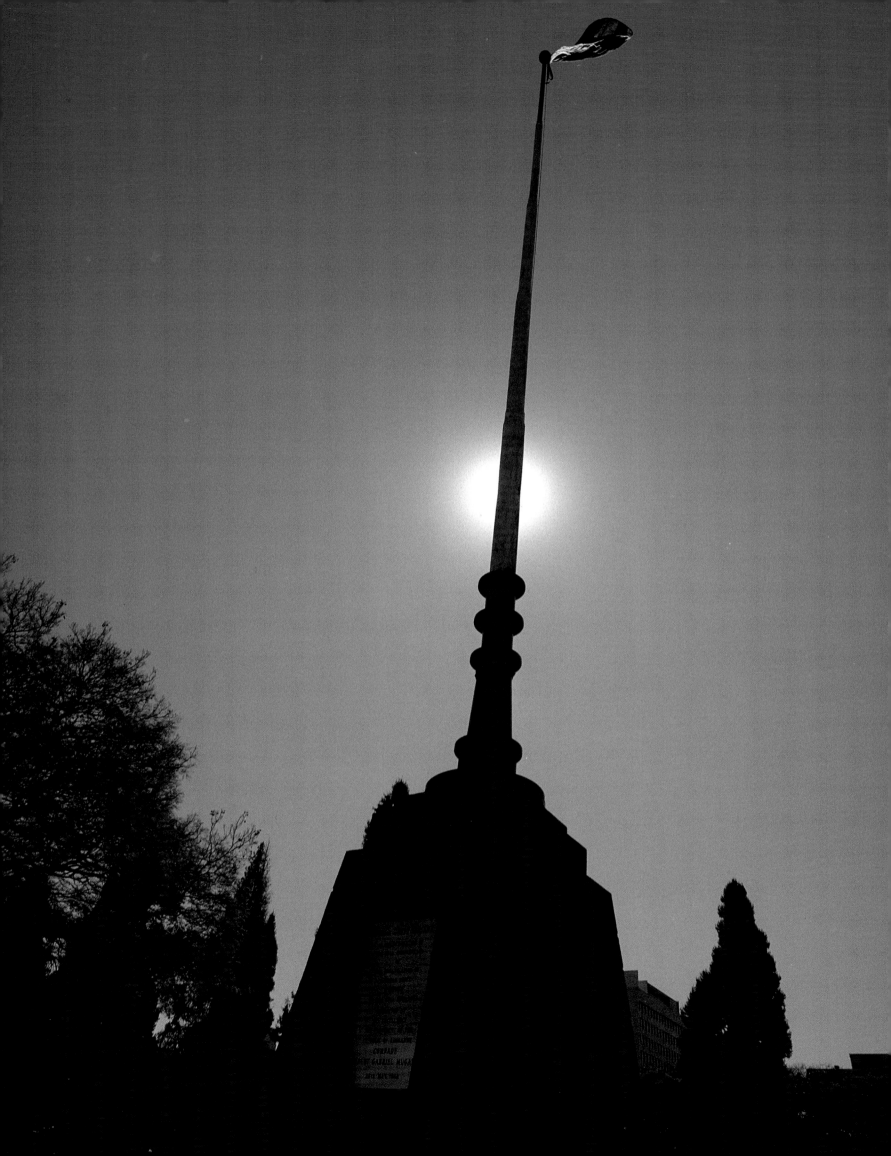

Opposite: Flagpole where Colonel Edward Pennefather, leader of the British South Africa Company's Pioneer Column made up of police and mercenaries, first raised the British flag on 12 September, 1890, in what was known as Cecil Square but is now African Unity Square — at the very heart of the capital of Zimbabwe.

To the south is the dirt road to Ngezi Recreational Park, a sixty-three-square kilometre nature reserve formed around the lake that was created by damming the Ngezi River — the northernmost of three rivers with the same name — in 1945.

With fishing and boating there are also nature trails through the wilderness areas, enabling wildlife such as antelope to be seen at close quarters. The sanctuary's birdlife is prolific and varied. There are many camp sites scattered along the lake shoreline, comfortable cottages, and caravan sites.

To the south of the main road just before Kadoma is John Mack Lake though who this commemorates is not recorded. But if any town can claim to be Zimbabwe's El Dorado, it must be Kadoma, born as a mining village in 1906. Although mining has declined in recent years, some of the country's largest and most profitable gold mines are still found in this area. But Kadoma does not depend on gold for its continued and increasing prosperity. It is a major collection centre for local cotton farmers and supports a large textiles manufacturing industry.

The multi-million dollar expansion to its attractive motel on the northern outskirts, remarked by the old steam engines that stand at the entrance, serves notice of the town's certainty in its future. It is around here too that one of the country's most popular private game ranches draws visitors all the year round.

The small village of Eiffel Flats, seven kilometres east of Kadoma, is a gold smelting centre on the spot where Dr. Starr Jameson pegged out claims to gold mines. When mining began in 1905 the village sprang up around it.

But it is the loop road north-west, through Golden Valley, and Chakari, to Chegutu that takes you into the heart of this golden bonanza. Miners in Golden Valley still hew the quartz and rocks in which the precious metal is found, and so maintain Zimbabwe's status as one of the world's major gold producers.

Chegutu, another mining and farm town thirty-four kilometres from Kadoma, is the last major centre before Harare, 106 kilometres to the north-east. From here the road runs through some of Zimbabwe's major tobacco farms.

The crop is the country's largest single foreign currency earner — realising around US$150 million a year in the second half of the 1980s. Grown long before the European settlers arrived, it was developed as a commercial crop in the first decade of this century.

Until UDI in 1965 Zimbabwe was the world's second-largest producer of tobacco, yielding more than 105,000 tonnes a year from around 1,500 farms and plantations. Since Independence production has constantly increased and the country now produces well above 110,000 tonnes a year. The main species is Virginia, but production of Burley has been increasing in recent years. Some oriental — Turkish — tobacco is also cultivated.

The US$6 million auction hall which was opened in Willowvale, Harare, in 1986 is the largest in the world. The amazing speed at which bids from national and overseas buyers are reeled off by the auctioneers astonishes all first-time visitors to these colourful auctions.

Some kilometres from Harare the Bulawayo road cuts between two of

Zimbabwe's finest manmade nature sanctuaries: Darwendale
Recreational Park on the east side, followed by Robert McIlwaine
Recreational Park to the west.

Darwendale Recreational Park was established in 1976 after damming
the Mhanyame River thirty kilometres downstream from the earlier
McIlwaine Dam.

The dam created eighty-one-square-kilometre Lake Robertson —
named after a former director of the Department of Irrigation — and is
now a major weekend resort for Harare citizens who come here to enjoy
watersports, fishing, and boating, all in what are largely natural, unspoilt
surroundings. Large mammals, particularly greater kudu, roam the
lake's woodland shores and the dam basin draws many species of water
birds.

The dam also led to the boring of Zimbabwe's longest tunnel; a large
water intake more than fifteen kilometres long which took four years to
complete. It funnels water to a station where it can be pumped upwards
and fed to Harare.

To the west of the road, some five kilometres beyond Lake Robertson's
shores, is sixteen-kilometre-long Lake McIlwaine, formed in 1952 when
the Mhanyame Poort Dam staunched the waters of the Mhanyame River.

Named after Sir Robert McIlwaine, an Irish-born lawyer who served in
Zimbabwe as a High Court Judge during colonial times, some twenty-
five square kilometres of foreshore and the thirty square kilometres of
water were established as a national park, its status changing to
recreational park later.

Sixteen square kilometres of the thickly-wooded shores are sanctuary
to buffalo, kudu, reedbuck, other antelope, baboon, many species of
monkey, and leopard. White rhino, giraffe, eland, wildebeest, and others
were introduced. There are more than 250 species of bird including
ostrich. More than twenty species of fish and Nile crocodile flourish in
the lake waters.

Despite the presence of the crocodiles, every Saturday and Sunday
dozens of water skiers cream the lake's waters behind their powerboats.
Within an hour's reach of the capital, McIlwaine is a popular weekend
playground for city residents.

It is at its best at midmorning when the bleached white sails of 100
yachts or more dot the sparkling blue waters. Private yachting and
powerboat clubs line the northern shores together with swimming pools
and play areas for children. There are also a hotel, tea garden, and
marina with lush lawns, and caravan and camp sites. On the southern
shore there's a delightful rest camp inside the game park where game
walks take place within a specified area. The lake's tigerfish and bream
offer good sport for anglers and licences are available from national
parks' staff or lakeshore establishments.

Forty kilometres eastward Harare's elegant new high-rise buildings
add yet another splendour to a city with arguable claim to be, if not the
most beautiful, certainly one of the world's most pleasant capitals. Its
centennial was marked on 12 September, 1990 — 100 years to the day
after the BSAC's 500-strong mercenary expedition, the Pioneer Column,
arrived at the end of their 600-kilometre, three-month trek from Fort Tuli.

Raising the British flag in what is now Cecil Square, the Commander,

*Opposite: Hyena are among the most efficient
predators in nature. Their powerful jaws can crack
any bones and almost anything else. They have been
known to eat anything from old leather saddles, to
dustbins and broomsticks.*

Left: Craft market in Harare.

Colonel Edward Pennefather, named the new settlement Fort Salisbury in honour of the incumbent British Prime Minister, the third Marquess of Salisbury. The site originally chosen for the fort was near Mount Hampden but when Pennefather surveyed the locality, he found that the land around the Kopje, a small granite outcrop rising out of the plain, was more suited to the expedition's needs.

The Mukuvisi river promised abundant water for the new town that would soon rise up on the open, fertile plain that stretched from the foot of the Kopje to the edge of the horizon. Such level land, with its granite bedrock, was ideal for the vision of the future city which Pennefather nurtured.

His faith was not misplaced. From the top of the Kopje with its landscaped garden and plaques commemorating the city's history, the visitor can enjoy a panoramic view of Harare today, a reality that more than honours the century-old dream of the Pioneer Column.

Laid out across several hundred square kilometres, with many islands of green — sports grounds, parks, and recreation areas — the capital's streets, lined with avenues of jacaranda and flame trees, are as broad and elegant as those of Bulawayo. Pleasant suburbs, with smart shopping centres, nostalgically named with such Anglo Saxon nomenclature as Kensington, Belgravia, Milton Park, and Belvedere, stretch in every direction. And although most of the original buildings have long been demolished to make way for new developments, many survive — some protected as national monuments or for their historic and architectural significance.

Dominating the city centre skyline, overlooking one and a half square

Above: Eighteenth hole of Harare Golf Club, venue for the annual Zimbabwe Open, one of the major events on the African Safari golf circuit.

kilometres of the main park, Harare Gardens, is the curved, slender profile of the eighteen-storey Monomotapa Hotel near the city's most modern landmark, the steel and glass Kangamombe House on the corner of Julius Nyerere Way and Samora Machel Avenue.

Yet many of the old names — Speke, Stanley, and Baker Avenues, for instance — remain and the English imprint is everywhere overlain, nowhere more so than in the pedestrian-only shopping mall right at the city's heart and in the window displays of the many chain stores. Despite severe foreign exchange restrictions, the windows offer contemporary fashions (virtually all designed and made in Zimbabwe) and a wide range of modern consumer goods.

Cecil Square, laid out patriotically in pre-Independence days in the shape of a Union Jack, remains the city's central motif. With magnificent trees, cascading fountain, and dazzling flower beds, this natural haven is bounded on one side by the 1960s Anglican Cathedral and the mellow Parliament Buildings and on the other by the modernistic lines of Meikles Hotel which in the 1960s replaced the seasoned early colonial elegance of the two-storey, verandahed original.

Parliament Buildings, where the democratically-elected black majority government meets, is a direct link with the history of Zimbabwe's colonization in the last decade of the last century. First begun in 1895, it was designed as a hotel — then known as Cecil Building — just a few metres from the spot where Pennefather and his pioneers raised the British flag.

The land which they claimed for the BSAC and themselves, in fact, was originally occupied by the Harava people, a Shona group under

Chief Mbare, after whom one of the city's main suburbs is named.

But when the pioneers arrived it was in the possession of Chief Gutsa and his warriors who had conquered the Harava, killing Chief Mbare. Although the first buildings were laid out at the foot of the Kopje, the marshy land there was unsuited to permanent buildings and most of the administration buildings were constructed closer to Cecil Square.

Fort Salisbury was a major pivot in Rhodes's masterplan for the annexation of Matabeleland and Mashonaland. Each civilian among the 500 pioneers in the column — the rest were BSAC police and regular troops — was given 1,250 hectares of land and the right to fifteen mining claims.

The Shona, like the Ndebele, bitterly resented this occupation and by 1894 the BSAC had built three forts on the slopes of the Kopje. The topmost one, Fort Leander, was fitted with a searchlight. Forced to labour on the new farms and in the new settlement through the introduction of the notorious hut tax, the Shona were then crippled in 1895 by smallpox and their herds wiped out by rinderpest, culminating

Above: Drivers and buggies take a tight corner at the Trotting Club track in an Harare suburb. Founded at the end of the 1950s it is the only trotting circuit in Africa. In 1989, more than fifty horses out of a total of 130 were in training for the regular thrice monthly meetings.

Above: Lush green straight of the Mashonaland Turf Club's Borrowdale course, headquarters of a multi-million dollar sports industry.

in a locust plaque the following year that decimated their crops. Almost simultaneous with the 1896 Ndebele uprising in Bulawayo, the Shona took to arms in the first of Zimbabwe's wars of liberation, *chimurenga*.

While Bulawayo's European settlers were retreating into a laager, Salisbury's new immigrants sought refuge in the town gaol which they fortified. There they waited, prepared for siege. But after six weeks, faced by superior arms and the arrival of troop reinforcements under Colonel Anderson, the Shona were forced to concede. Their spiritual leaders, Mbuya Nehanda and Kaguvi, were taken prisoner, tried and convicted. They were hanged in 1897, the year in which Salisbury attained municipal status under the leadership of its first mayor, W. E. Fairbridge.

At the time of the *chimurenga* the new hotel, commissioned by two carpet-baggers from the Kimberley gold fields, Robert Snodgrass and Daniel Mitchell, was just an empty shell. Nonetheless, with the onset of the rains late in 1896, Colonel Anderson requisitioned the building as barracks for his men.

Two years later when Snodgrass and Mitchell ended their

partnership, the building — dining room, billiard hall, and eighteen bedrooms — was still unfinished and the BSAC, which had loaned the partners £7,000 to build it, took it over with the intention of turning it into the new town's General Post Office.

Within weeks, however, a Legislative Council to rule over this 'new territory' was established and the hotel's dining room was earmarked as the assembly chamber, the bar and lounge as legislative offices, and the upstairs rooms — though some were still without floors — as government offices.

The Public Works Department were assigned to complete the work and the first meeting of the new Legislative Council on 15 May, 1899, took place surrounded by builders, carpenters, plumbers, and all the paraphernalia of building work. The meeting coincided with the arrival of the railway. Three years later, with the completion of the line to Bulawayo in 1902, Salisbury was proclaimed the new capital.

Two decades later when Rhodesia was proclaimed a self-governing colony, the chamber was too small for the first opening of Parliament. It was held instead in the capital's Princess Hall. But after acrimonious debates about building a new Parliament, the members decided to expand and improve Cecil Building.

In the years between there have been many more developments culminating with expansions in 1969 which elevated the building to six storeys. It was here eleven years later, on 14 May, 1980, that President Caanan Banana performed the first state opening of independent Zimbabwe's Parliament and where, late in 1989, Zimbabwe's 100 MPs voted to merge the two-chamber Westminster model Parliament into one house in 1990, abolishing the unelected forty-seat Senate for an enlarged single chamber of 150 MPs, of whom 120 will contest their seats in the General Elections. The other thirty seats will be taken by the

Above: Cricket on the grounds of Harare Club where an England eleven played the national side in March 1990. Keen to become a Test playing nation, Zimbabwe has already produced the most outstanding batsman of England's first-class county game — Worcestershire's Graeme Hick.

Opposite: Verdant lawns and flower beds in the two square kilometres of colourful eighty-year-old Harare Gardens which boasts bowling greens, bandstand, open air theatre, and children's playground. In the background is the Monomotapa Hotel, built in 1974.

Above: Colourful fruit stall in Harare's popular Mbare Market.

governors of Zimbabwe's eight provinces, ten traditional chiefs, and twelve members nominated by the President.

Yet, almost a century after Snodgrass and Mitchell decided to give shape to their grand vision of an elegant hotel, the interior of Cecil Building was still surprisingly intact — with the original doors, windows, floors, and ceilings still in place. But as Harare prepared to celebrate the centennial of its founding as Fort Salisbury, the Cecil Building's historic role was drawing to a close. Plans for a new Parliamentary complex on top of the Kopje were well-advanced. Conservationists, however, were hopeful that the old Parliament Buildings would be preserved as a national monument. Certainly as the one visible continuity between Zimbabwe's original colonization and its first decade of Independence, it is perhaps the most significant building — architecturally and historically — in the country after the ruins of Great Zimbabwe.

Many historic monuments, mostly of a colonial nature, retain their place in Harare's architectural legacy: the staff where Pennefather raised the British flag marks the entrance to Cecil Square; cenotaphs to

*Above: When the jacaranda bloom between
September and October, Harare's wide streets
become a sea of mauve.*

the dead of two world wars dominate Harare Gardens (and also a
1913 drinking fountain commemorating Britain's King George V); and
the city's excellent Queen Victoria Museum is now the headquarters
of the National Museum.

Flanked by the city's Les Brown swimming pool on one side, and
the National Art Gallery on the other, Harare Gardens is a treasured
recreation area of leafy avenues, an open air theatre, bandstand,
children's playground, bowling greens, and a miniature model of the
Victoria Falls.

Other colonial-style legacies seen in Harare are the verdant
Borrowdale racecourse, centre of the Turf Club of Mashonaland's
multi-million dollar enterprise which includes Tote and offcourse
betting shops, and the equally verdant and abundant golf courses,
cricket, bowls, tennis, hockey, and rugby grounds.

But soccer is the national sport and Harare's Chinese-built National
Sports Stadium is one of the showpieces of Africa — as is the futuristic
Harare International Conference Centre, the continent's largest, clad in
burnished gold panelling. Close to it is the spacious showground of

the Zimbabwe Agricultural Society, founded in 1899, and the setting for the colourful Harare Agricultural Show held each August. Nearby is the National Sports Centre.

Top golfers walk the fairways of Royal Harare Golf Club each year during the Zimbabwe Open, one of the major events in the African Safari circuit. Though seemingly mundane from the fence, the landscaping of this course when seen from the patio, overlooking both the first tee and eighteenth hole, is a tribute to both designer and nature's form.

Opposite the club are the spacious grounds of State House, containing what was both the Prime Minister's official residence and State House, the residence of the President. Now both offices have been combined, the President occupies State House which was built in 1910, and which in the years since has been considerably extended.

Beyond the plant research experimental station which borders State House grounds stand almost seven square kilometres of land, reserved as a recreation area in 1902 and transformed since 1962 into the National Botanical Gardens under Dr. Hyram Wilder. Half of this area displays typical plants of Zimbabwe's woodlands. Other areas contain a selection of plants typical of the African continent, including rare and endangered species. Elsewhere exotic species from South America, India, Australia, and the Far East, flourish.

The Gardens are contiguous to the splendid National Archives, which was built in 1961 and is a repository of Zimbabwe's pre-, colonial, and post-colonial history with more than 40,000 books and many rare and precious manuscripts and documents.

And in one of the streets close to Harare's inner sanctum stand the first

Above: Spectacular rock formations of the Epworth Balancing Rocks, Harare, which was long a privately-run attraction, are now in the charge of the National Parks and Wildlife Department.

Above: Stone carvings such as these representations from granite and serpentine, one of the country's indigenous rocks, have earned Zimbabwe's sculptors international acclaim. Of the world's ten leading stone sculptors in 1990, seven were from Zimbabwe.

jacaranda trees planted in the city, while in an eastern suburb, long a source of curiosity for city dwellers, the spectacular Epworth Balancing Rocks, once a privately-run attraction now part of the national parks and reserves, provide novice rock climbers with a splendid summer evening challenge.

Harare's vibrant African ambience is best experienced in the downtown Mbare, Graniteside, and Arcadia suburbs where craft markets display a fascinating range of traditional indigenous carvings, fabric, basketwork, metalwork, and agricultural produce.

Here, too, in the adjacent Workington industrial area Zimbabwe's colonial past is still present in such prosaic place names as Birmingham, Glasgow, Barrow, and Plymouth roads.

Yet all these vestiges of colonialism are overshadowed by the magnificence of the ceremonial Independence arches which greet the visitor on the road from the airport and by the moving splendour of Heroes' Acre, a ceremonial burial ground on a forested ridge four kilometres west of the city centre, where the martyrs who laid down their lives for freedom, and those who have died since Independence in the service of their nation, are buried.

As the first decade of independence closed, Harare was developing swiftly. With a population of around one million people, new factories and suburban estates were extending the city's peripheries but careful planning ensured that the spaciousness and cleanliness of broad and sunny streets would endure all change — to add more than a measure of delight not only to its ever-increasing number of citizens but to the ever-increasing number of visitors it welcomes each year.

5. The Kingdom of Ophir

Three hundred kilometres south of Harare are two symbols that, together, illustrate the past, present, and future of free Zimbabwe. No more than thirty kilometres separate them but they are worlds apart in their significance. One defines both its modern spirit and ancient character. The other is silent witness to the imperial ambitions of Cecil Rhodes, and of the lust for glory and riches that drove him to his conquests.

The way north that Rhodes's mercenary Pioneer Column followed a century ago is marked by the chain of forts — four in all — that they built along their route. The first of these is Fort Tuli which stands on Zimbabwe's border with South Africa. The second stands on Clipsham Farm on the perimeter of what is now Masvingo, the oldest town in the country. This is where Rhodes's white conquistadores arrived on 17 August, 1890, and at once signified their intentions by building Fort Victoria.

Just twenty-six kilometres from its portals stands the ancient city-state of Great Zimbabwe which is significant for two reasons. For 300 years or so, known to the outside world only by legend, it inspired stories that it was the Biblical kingdom of Ophir which Sheba visited; a myth that persisted even after its 'discovery' in 1867.

It was also the touchstone that inspired the war of liberation and gave its name to the nation, testimony to the centuries-old civilization that flourished there long before the arrival of the European. Its ruins, and the ancient works of art found there, encompass a cultural and architectural heritage unsurpassed almost anywhere south of the Sahara — and seal an implicit promise for the future. Not only does it contain all that is most sacred of the past, it also bequeaths to future generations the legacy for which so many gave their lives.

Fort Victoria marks where and when that ages-old civilization was finally confronted, contained, and ruthlessly suppressed. It lies close to a winding twelve-kilometre pass through which the column marched, fearing it was a dead end and that they might be ambushed. Such was their relief at finding their way safely through that they gave it the name of Providential Pass.

Within months the fortress and the small settlement that sprang up around it — known as Fort Victoria until Independence — became an important staging post on the road to Fort Salisbury, and a major mining centre.

After only two years, however, the town was moved to a new site some five kilometres from the original location and a permanent fort, with narrow embrasures, was built at the centre. Bricks were fashioned and baked on the banks of the Mucheke River and carried to the site on ox wagons operated by a trio of transport riders from the Transvaal, Tom Meikle and his brothers John and Stewart, who went on to found one of the country's wealthiest dynasties. You can still see the remains of this fort and two of the original watchtowers, one of them now a small museum.

It was there, one year later, in July, 1893, that the same Dr. Jameson whose body lies close to that of Rhodes in the Matobo Hills, summoned a force of Ndebele warriors. Without provocation, he then ordered the BSAC contingent to attack them. The skirmish left between thirty and

Previous pages: Arid Shona communal lands. Under the British South Africa Company the most fertile land was taken for European settlement and the remainder designated as Tribal Trust Lands.

Above: Open air market in the mining town of Zvishavane.

fifty Ndebele dead, and sparked the uprising that culminated in the razing of Bulawayo. And the sackcloth and ashes of colonial domination.

Forming a mercenary force to follow up the attack and put down Lobengula and his armies once and for all, Jameson offered each volunteer large farms in Matabeleland and the right to stake a given number of mining claims, together with a share of cattle from the Ndebele herds. Known as the 'Victoria Rangers' the mercenaries then rode out in pursuit of the retreating *impi* to conquer Lobengula.

At the end, many of his warriors dead, his capital in ashes, Lobengula fled north and Jameson and the 'Rangers' established the British settlement at Bulawayo.

Effectively, this relegated Fort Victoria to an insignificant role in the formative, bloodstained years of Rhodes's new colony. For with Matabeleland opened to Rhodes's mercenaries and settlers, the town fell into swift decline.

Even ten years later its European population numbered only slightly more than 300, mainly settlers and prospectors (of which less than a third were women), who were often so strapped for cash that the town's first postmaster, George Bowen, who also doubled as the Mining Commissioner, let them have their postage stamps on credit.

For all that, however, Fort Victoria had the style and stamina of a gold rush town with grizzled, bush-hardened veterans of the African heat drifting into town to slake their thirst at the 'Thatched House'.

Among the most colourful of these characters, as many a man discovered to his cost, was 'French Marie' who, dressed in breeches and boots and carrying a sjambok, was built like the proverbial brick privy and swore like a trooper. French Marie, who started the Green Rose Mine, developed several other claims before retiring to farm at Borrowdale, near Harare.

It was also the place where the Meikle brothers opened the enterprise on which the family's fortunes were founded, the first of what became a chain of hotels and stores throughout the country — a crude store built out of whisky cases and roofed with tarpaulin.

In 1914 Tom Meikle bought the 'Thatched House', knocked it down, and replaced it with the Victoria Hotel which still occupies the site. And the present-day successor to Meikle's original shop now covers almost one hectare of ground and dominates Masvingo's main street.

Fort Victoria, which was elevated to town status in 1926 and which became a municipality in 1953, is today capital of Masvingo Province and still an important farm and mining centre — and the springboard to the lowveld.

The second Fort is the building you see on the road to Great Zimbabwe, the fabled site of the Biblical Ophir, the land where Queen Sheba came for gold and ivory to decorate the temple of Solomon. A legend based on the wild and wonderful assumptions of sixteenth-century Portuguese travellers who, although they never visited the state-city, heard many tales of its citadels and fortresses, its immense wealth and far-ranging power.

For almost a century these mysterious ruins acted as a magnet, drawing adventurers and archaeologists from all parts of the world. Most of these early 'explorers' refused to believe that any African culture could be responsible for such sophistication and most claimed the ruins were connected to the Old Testament — to the Queen of Sheba, or the Phoeniceans, or the Sabeans, or Ophir. And, indeed, the many gold beads and ornaments found at Great Zimbabwe testify that it was the centre of a gold trading empire.

But they have no link with the Bible, Sheba, or Solomon. Sheba's Axuma is the ancient city of Axum in Ethiopia's Tigray Province, but Great Zimbabwe — the ancient city that the Portuguese declared was Axuma — was, however, the powerhouse of a unique southern African economy. In fact, the truth about these ruins, where the spirit of the national persona seeps from every granite stone, is far more incredible than the wildest fantasies.

The kingdom's magnificent capital, set in a rugged kopje-strewn valley was built by a civilization which first flowered more than 1,000 years ago and flourished for more than seven centuries.

Now a World Heritage Site, these are the most spectacular remains of any human settlement in Africa south of the Sahara, and also the largest, and most intact, of more than 150 ruined fortified towns and villages found throughout the country.

Since Independence, the natural vegetation of the vleis and hills around the ruins has been restored and exotics, such as the Australian eucalyptus introduced by the Europeans, removed. Nearby are four hectares of aloe gardens and a hotel.

Perhaps the only thing that remains unchanged is the natural fauna. The ruins abound with wildlife such as the greater kudu, bushbuck, duiker, steinbok, klipspringer, leopard, and baboon and among the many birds that inhabit the ruins and the trees are hornbills, green pigeons, freckled nightjars, and purple-crested herons.

For many years, however, the full extent and significance of these

Above: Old steam engine outside Masvingo Civic Centre honours the town's early, rumbustious history when it was known as Fort Victoria, the place from which Dr. Leander Starr Jameson engineered the defeat of Lobengula.

Above: Entrance to the hill complex which was the royal residence of Great Zimbabwe. The massive walls were not built for defence but as showpieces of the city-state's power.

Overleaf: Great Zimbabwe forms the most significant ancient ruins in sub-Saharan Africa. Seen from the hill complex, the ruins of the city state's Great Enclosure are encircled by a wall which has a circumference of more than quarter of a kilometre and contains more than 15,000 tonnes of granite rock.

ruins was not readily appreciated. Indeed, from the time that Adam Renders, a renegade American sailor thought to be the first known white man to see them, set eyes on the ruins in about 1867 they were despoliated and plundered for almost four decades. Priceless treasures and relics were uprooted and hauled away with impunity.

Renders never made his discovery known for he married the daughter of an African chief and remained in the area until his death in 1881. It was left to Carl Mauch, a German adventurer who arrived at the site on 5 September, 1871, to confirm to the world the existence of the ruins.

Despite his firm and erroneous belief that this was Ophir, the credit for much of what is known today must rest with the diligent Mauch who was the first to describe them accurately (indeed, the only one to describe them in their pristine state for the subsequent plunder destroyed much of what he saw). Never a plunderer, Mauch's one concern was the preservation of the ruins and he recorded much essential data in great detail, including descriptions of the religious ceremonies, both past and present, that took place.

First occupied in the eighth century AD, Great Zimbabwe evolved from a small settlement into an immensely powerful state, ruled over by a succession of kings whose influence spread throughout what is now Zimbabwe.

Radio-carbon dating and archaeological finds suggest that this royal capital reached its greatest eminence between the eleventh and fifteenth centuries AD when it dominated a large upland area and controlled the gold trade to the coast.

Left: Great Zimbabwe's Great Enclosure is dominated by this thirty-six foot high conical tower but its purpose remains a mystery yet to be resolved.

Below: Outer wall of Great Zimbabwe's hill complex looks out over the once fertile plains below.

During those four centuries when Europe languished in its dark ages, most of the stone houses, *'dzimba dzemagwe'*, were built by the Karanga dynasty, those ancestors of the present Shona people, who ruled the *Dzemagwe* kingdom.

The centrepiece, a huge elliptical wall dominated by a solid stone, conical tower, sometimes higher than thirty feet and more than five metres thick — with a circumference of more than 250 metres — encircled the impressive capital. The earliest of these walls enclosed what were sacred sites and at its peak the city, the largest of any in Africa at that time, had something like 20,000 citizens.

Perhaps most fascinating of all is that the intricate complex has endured as long as 700 years without mortar as all were built using the dry-stone technique for constructing walls.

Evidence of the scope and size of this ancient nation's trade is dramatic. Over the years excavations have uncovered articles from China, India, and Asia. Of all these finds, however, the most intriguing — eight delicately-carved soapstone birds which have since been adopted as the national symbol of independent Zimbabwe — had nothing to do with trade or wealth, or foreign countries.

Yet, clearly, its wealth and power as a trading state grew and developed as a result of the Arab gold trade. But although its development and the extent of its wealth and influence is well

Right: One of the original soapstone birds found in the ruins of Great Zimbabwe and now part of the national flag and coat of arms.

documented the reason for Great Zimbabwe's sudden decline in the fifteenth century remains an enigma. Almost overnight it ceased to be of any importance although small groups continued to live there for three centuries or more.

When the kopje and the valley were first settled the area was an island of green, even during the dry winter months, because of the unusually moderate climate. Moreover, as the kingdom grew in size and importance, the granite rocks of the surrounding hills proved to be ideal for building.

Some experts believe that most of the people were forced to move elsewhere after destroying the forest and wood cover and overgrazing the surrounding grasslands. Whatever the reason, the civilization went into a decline from which it never recovered. What they left behind, however, after occupying what is now Zimbabwe's premier national monument for seven centuries, is stunning testament to the wealth, sophistication, and stability of the *Dzimbagwe* civilization.

Sprawled across seven-and-a-half square kilometres of valley and hilltop are the remains of three major stone edifices: the hill complex, great enclosure or Great House (*Imba Huru*), and the valley complex.

Above: Grinding flour with traditional pestle in a Shona village.

Seen from a distance, bathed in the gentle sunlight of an early November afternoon, as galleons of cloud chase each other across the sky, the walls that curve so gracefully along the contour of the great whaleback kopje seem almost sensuous; as if moulding and flexing themselves to each rise and fall of the ridge.

From the gate you follow a trail over lush meadowlands to the foot of the kopje where the only way up the face of the almost sheer 300 foot cliff was by a precipitous stairway cut through the rock. Toward the summit, it tapers sharply and becomes so narrow that many have to turn sideways to continue. For today's visitors, however, a new approach has been made around the east of the hill — wider and much more gentle of incline.

Breathless now, the solid masonry of the wall stands in front of you with a slim portcullis for entry. Step through this and the walls that surround you seem to breathe still of all those yesterdays. Despite the deserted enclosures, it's easy enough to imagine yourself back in the twelfth century.

The ambience is mesmeric. Dragonflies hover over the rocks and skinks and lizards dart among the cracks and crannies of the ancient walls causing images of those long ago days to playback constantly in the mind as the echoes of forgotten sounds and movements whisper and murmur on the gentle breeze.

In style and content there is no other architecture like this. It is unique, rooted in the land which gave it life, a startling osmosis growing with splendid spontaneity from the rocks on which the edifices stand, drawing this ancient granite, split by the hot sun and freezing nights of the highveld, into the soul of its existence, so that rock and structure become as one.

Everywhere, in a syntax of harmonious curves and contours that draw their inspiration from the hills around, these walls endow a sense of liberation. No citadel this, though, for perhaps unique in the world all those years ago these walls were never built for defence.

This is where, splendidly aloof from their citizenry, gazing down from on high at the greatest city-state of its time and place, the ruling kings lived; and where it all began for this is the oldest surviving part of Great Zimbabwe.

Close by, on the same ridge, stand many smaller enclosures of ritualistic and historic significance — one a recess, another an ironstone cave, a third for smelting, and a fourth, the ritual enclosure where most of the eight Zimbabwe Birds were discovered.

Below, lying in the valley at the southern foot of the hill, the largest and best preserved remains, known as the great enclosure, were built some time after the hill complex. The massive outer wall, which in places stands as high as thirty-five feet, is a quarter of a kilometre in circumference. Shaped roughly like an ellipse, its widest point is more than 100 metres across.

It contains more than 15,000 tonnes of granite blocks making it the largest single ancient structure in sub-Saharan Africa and it needs no imagination to measure the scale of achievement this represented in a city of only 20,000 people. Not just for the proportions of the work alone, but also for the extreme level of skill that the masons displayed in shaping and laying the stones; especially the two-foot wide, eighty-eight metre long decorative chevron band that runs along the top of the massive exterior wall.

The pattern, seen elsewhere in Africa on walls and doors or clothing but never on this scale, pays homage to 'the snake of fertility'. It is a votive symbol designed, in this instance, to ensure a continuous line of dynastic Karanga rulers for the royal palace above.

Through the centuries the quality of the masonry constantly improved. The first walls, built of uneven stone, look irregular. But those built 200 years later have great symmetry. The stone matches and is laid in straight, even lines, each level set fractionally back from the one below so that the wall appears to lean inward, providing equilibrium and stability. Around this time drainage systems were developed, stairways became sinuous, expressive works of grace as well as functional steps, and doorways were given rounded jambs.

All this was designed to emphasise the power of the nation — a salute to the unity of the people and the dignity and glory of the ruling dynasty — not to defend the city-state.

The great enclosure was such an expression, built to house the women of the royal family. It is dominated by a magnificent conical tower, a solid stone structure rising more than thirty-six feet with a base circumference of five metres. The top of the tower was originally decorated with two rows carved in a dog tooth pattern but since the rulers and citizens left no known written records — neither inscriptions nor documents — the purpose of the tower remains a mystery.

Beyond the great enclosure stretch the remains of the dry-stone enclosures that make up the valley complex, believed to have housed lesser court dignitaries and other important people. Despite the earlier plunder, this site has yielded many valuable relics and artefacts.

Most of the clay-and-gravel thatched huts in these enclosures were joined by stone walls each with its own platform where the wealth of the individual family — its pots and precious metal (gold and copper, in particular) were displayed. The peasantry lived outside the walled enclosures in similar huts.

Almost every entrance to the enclosures is marked by an empty slot. These were for the city's totems — pillars of wood or stone carved with abstract designs or images of reptiles, animals, and birds, some grouped together. The best of the wood carvings were enclosed in sheaths of beaten copper and gold, but all this wealth of sculpture has tragically vanished, now lost to all but the imagination.

Of the few pieces that survived, the most significant and important of the stone totems are the eight carved birds (it is believed that originally there were ten). About thirteen inches high, they adorned the tops of three-foot-high columns. What they represented, however, is not known. The evidence either never existed or was destroyed.

One researcher believes the eastern enclosure was used for religious ceremonies where the Karanga prayed to *Mwari* to bring relief from drought and other disasters. Indeed, one excavation uncovered the remains of more than 1,300 head of cattle: evidence of the wealth of the community for most of these were probably killed as religious sacrifices.

Mauch concluded that between every two and three years there was a large gathering after the harvest, followed by the sacrifice of several black cattle to appease the tribal spirits for in the Shona faith such prayers are not direct but through the spirits of dead ancestors.

The ceremonies were presided over by one of the tribal priests, helped by two virgins. During the ceremony one cow was burnt alive in the royal citadel and an ox was roasted and eaten. A third beast, also

Above: White rhino in Lake Kyle game sanctuary. Second-largest of all land animals, weighing between 2,000 and 4,000 kilos, it is much more docile than the black rhino. It was slaughtered out of existence in this region in the last century but, reintroduced in 1967, it now flourishes.

Above: Flanked by magnificent hills, Lake Kyle is sanctuary to many creatures — including the greatest variety of antelope species found anywhere in Zimbabwe — among them the world's tallest creature. Giraffe have a complex biosystem that monitors and regulates their blood pressure allowing them to lower their heads to drink without blacking out.

an ox, was then killed some distance from the temple, and its carcase left for scavengers and vultures.

Later, the priest entered a sacred cave where he sprinkled beer and prayed to God, *Mwari*, to heal the sick and assure good health for the people. Returning from the cave, there were more sacrifices. The cattle thus offered were suffocated by choking them with their own dung and taken into the bush.

If the scavengers, vultures, and predators feasted on them overnight it was a sign that the spirits were pleased and there was a great celebration with people clapping their hands and fanfares of horns.

Seldom seen by white men, the Shona still offer sacrifices. It is traditional when a grandfather dies to name a black bull or ox after him. Later, when the grandfather is believed to want to claim the bull, a diviner is consulted. If the signs are propitious, the sacrifice is made.

Tied to a tree, the bull is hammered unconscious by the eldest son-in-law who then cuts its throat, draining the blood into a gourd. Other members of the family remove the head and place it in a shrine and then butcher the beast, sharing the choicest cuts among the man's children and grandchildren. The rest is served to everyone present.

Many archaeologists consider that the Zimbabwe birds represent dead rulers. The fact that many Shona describe them as tombstones supports the suggestion.

Whatever their symbolic meaning to the Karanga dynasty and people, however, they remain a priceless representation of a unique past — and, perhaps more important, of a hopeful future. Indeed, one now serves as the country's national totem and, in the minds of most Zimbabweans, it is the most cherished emblem of the struggle for independence. Highly stylised, it has been incorporated into the country's flag and national coat of arms.

Above: Many granite kopjes guard the Masvingo-Johannesburg road.

Initially, four of these carvings were discovered within the eastern enclosure of the hill complex, the royal palace, on a series of manmade platforms. Although the carvings follow essentially the same pattern, the ring and chevron markings vary, making it possible to identify each bird.

Carved from a soft green-grey soapstone common to central and northern Zimbabwe, one archaeologist said they were the 'only sculptures of any size or complexity, or displaying any attempt at representation, from Great Zimbabwe or any south-central African prehistoric site'.

Yet within years all were removed. The first was taken by Transvaal hunter Willie Posselt who visited the ruins in 1889. Uncaringly, Posselt simply hacked one bird from its pillar and carried it back to the Transvaal where he offered it to President Kruger. He showed no interest but Rhodes did. He paid fifty dollars and mounted it on a pedestal in the library of his Groote Schuur home. Later, cement replicas were placed on the gateposts of Dalham Hall, his English home.

Eight other birds were looted after Posselt's discovery. Six went to Cape Town, one to Bulawayo, and the head of one to Harare while the the body went to Berlin in Germany.

The bird in Bulawayo, unweathered and fresh from the sculptor's chisel, was apparently never erected. It is believed to have been the 'tombstone' intended for the king who died shortly before the 1831 invasion of the Zwangendaba which finally destroyed Great Zimbabwe.

A perspective of time and place helps provide an appreciation not only of the significance of Great Zimbabwe as a cultural heritage but also the scale of its achievement at a time when medieval Europe was yet to emerge from its dark ages. Already, on the other side of the hemisphere, Great Zimbabwe was a truly civic community with clear

Above: Sugarcane ripens in the 160 square kilometres of the giant Hippo Valley Sugar Estate near Chiredzi on the lowveld. Until the 1950s this area of the lowveld was uninhabitable, tsetse-fly infested scrub.

rankings of authority, and concern for all citizens.

By then the site had been occupied for at least two millenniums if not more. Stone Age peoples left behind evidence of their occupation in the form of rock paintings. By AD 300 pottery and ironwork had been developed and some 700 years or so after this cattle were grazing the land, crops were cultivated, and trade with Arabia, through the East African coast, had started to develop. Glass beads found on site confirm this.

Soon the pace of development accelerated. The cattle herds increased dramatically and it is easy to understand why the people believed in the potency of these sacrifices as Great Zimbabwe grew and prospered through the centuries.

It became the capital of a great commercial empire with its own iron ore mines and smithies, a militant army that produced much plunder, tributary chiefs, and traders who dealt in gold, copper, iron, ivory, cotton, and cattle, much of which was carried long distances for there was little gold or metal around the capital. These were the basis of a flourishing trade with Arabia and Asia in return for finished cloth, pottery, beads, and other ornaments.

The carved birds represented the zenith of this great civilization which, like all great civilizations and for whatever reason, went into swift and traumatic decline. By AD 1500 it had lost all power and importance.

Those carvings outside the country were returned soon after Independence at the request of the newly-independent Zimbabwe government and are now on display in the site museum, along with artefacts excavated from the area. There's also an interpretative display of the prehistory and history of Great Zimbabwe and a model of the city at the height of its power.

For most visitors, this serves as acknowledgement of the proud and disciplined civilization that went before but which was plundered unheedingly by the new colonialists.

Looking north-east from the ruins of the hill complex, however, you can see, eight kilometres in the distance, a beneficial legacy of colonial rule that serves as both recreational resort and natural asset.

To reach Lake Kyle, however, you have to follow the Birchenough Road out of Masvingo, past the stunning chapel built during World War II by Italian prisoners of war, complete with golden frescos and murals reminiscent of the Sistine chapel.

Most of these are the work of one man, a peacetime civil engineer. The chapel is also a mausoleum for seventy-one prisoners who died during their captivity. It lies about halfway between the town and the right turn that leads some twenty-five kilometres to the lake which, though a minnow by comparison to Lake Kariba, is the country's second-largest. It was formed at the confluence of the Mshagashe and Mtirikwe rivers when they were dammed in 1960 to feed the vast irrigation schemes needed to develop the Triangle and Hippo Valley

Above: Magnificent frescos and murals decorate the interior of the Italian Chapel near Masvingo built by Italian prisoners of war during World War II as a mausoleum for seventy-one colleagues who died during internment.

Above: Shona drummer.

sugar and citrus estates in the humid lowveld to the south. More than 300 metres wide, the dam rises 207 feet from the bed of a narrow granite gorge.

Much of the land around the lake forms the 169 square kilometres of Kyle Recreational Park. In 1989, however, years of drought had reduced the lake to about one-fifth of its original ninety-one square kilometres.

But whether swollen or shrunk, nothing can diminish the beauty of its setting. The park lies in a landscape broken by ranges of weathered granite hills and deep ravines. To the west the boundary is formed by the sensual outline of the Beza Range. In the east rise the spectacular, thickly-wooded Nyuni Mountains.

The eighty-nine square kilometre game reserve supports the greatest number of antelope species found in any national park or game sanctuary in the country, including wildebeest, greater kudu, nyala, bushbuck, eland, reedbuck, impala, sable, oribi, duiker, steinbok, blesbok, and Lichtenstein's hartebeest. Most visitors follow the many nature trails on foot or by pony to study the wildlife which also includes zebra, wart hog, ostrich, white rhino, buffalo, and giraffe.

The white rhino were imported into the reserve from Natal. The first calf since the species was wiped out in the area during the last century was born in 1967. The nyala were also introduced.

Lake Kyle supports abundant hippopotamus and crocodile and around the lake, and on its many islands, the bird life is prolific and includes nesting colonies of cormorants and herons. When full, the lake is an ideal water resort with fishing, yachting, power-boating and water-skiing. It is considered to offer the best black bass fishing in the country. Other fish include tilapia, yellowfish, and bottlenose.

The water released downstream flows into a holding dam, then onto a weir and, finally, into the Triangle Canal which feeds the lowveld plantations. By road, the journey to Chiredzi, the smart new 'capital' of this lush cornucopia, is much longer. It first travels out of Masvingo some distance south along the Beitbridge-Johannesburg road, through a landscape of massive and dramatic granite kopjes, before turning east along the arrow-straight road that runs through the sweltering lowlands. After the first rains drivers at night face a blizzard of 'sausage flies', termites, and myriad other winged insects that take the rains as their cue to hatch, often in such large numbers that they eventually block the windscreen.

The giant Triangle sugar mill and Hippo Valley have turned Chiredzi from a sleepy hamlet into perhaps Zimbabwe's fastest-growing town. Little more than thirty years ago all this area was a monotonously flat, bush-tangled, tsetse fly-infested wilderness dotted with baobab trees and choked with scrub.

Intensive tsetse control programmes over an extensive area, reaching beyond the Mozambique border, eradicated the fly and farm developers noted the climate was ideal for citrus production — if only there were enough water. In 1956, tapping the waters of the Runde river, Hippo Valley Estate established its first citrus plantation. Three years later water from Lake Kyle came onstream and the plantation expanded.

Lacking sufficient domestic or export markets, however, the company reduced the amount of land devoted to citrus growing and turned to large scale sugar growing. Hippo Valley now covers 160 square kilometres of land of which in 1989 more than 100 square kilometres were covered by sugarcane. The amount under cultivation is governed by water levels and Zimbabwe has yet to recover from the severe droughts which reduced Lake Kyle to a fifth of its usual size.

Neat roads slice through this massive development with more than twenty model workers' estates, schools, and health clinics. The mill is capable of producing more than 10,000 tonnes of sugar a day.

The cane is cut after it has been burnt. It makes harvesting and handling easier. All across the plantation, great tongues of flame climb dozens of feet into the sky during the cutting season as the fires rage through each chosen block. Cane from the sister Mkwaseni Estate, some thirty kilometres to the north-east, is also processed at the factory and many outgrowers depend on it for their livelihood.

Some private game ranches, a few with their own motels, flourish nearby and game ranching has become a major growth industry — particularly ostrich and crocodile farming. Demand for ostrich meat is experiencing a boom in the west because of its low cholesterol content and the leather industry's demand for ostrich skin is insatiable. Each bird produces between five and seven kilos of meat fit for human consumption.

The chicks are hatched in sterile conditions in giant incubators and grow like weeds. But they are not as hardy. These giant, flightless birds are prone to many blights and diseases.

There's a similar demand for crocodile products with the soft belly skin fetching around US$7 dollars a centimetre. Culled while still young, the belly pelt averages around thirty centimetres bringing between US$200-250 each. Meat and other by products make crocodile farming an extremely lucrative industry. As part of their agreement with the conservation authorities, the farm also restocks rivers and lakes.

Civil engineer Ian Rule, who built dams and irrigation works before he quit to become general manager of Chiredzi Wildlife Investments, said they were planning to farm other wild game species. The ranch also trains safari guides, hunters, and conservationists and quotes as its philosophy, 'If you don't put a price tag on a species, it's dead'.

There's plenty of room for expansion. The ranch has ninety-six square kilometres of land available although the crocodile and ostrich ranch only covers a small area of this.

Sixty-five miles north of Chiredzi, along a gravel road, lies the unspoilt beauty of thirty-five-square-kilometre Manjirenji Recreational Park, a little visited haven encompassing Lake Manjirenji, formerly Lake McDougall, where the fish are said to be uncommonly canny.

And some forty kilometres south of Chiredzi lies one of Zimbabwe's great wilderness retreats, 4,964 square kilometres that represent Gonarezhou National Park, its south-east boundary drawn along the Mozambique border.

Its existence also highlights the perennial dilemma between wildlife conservation and economic development. One of Zimbabwe's major foreign exchange earners is the ranching industry and in this region beef and buffalo are in virtual confrontation as the European Economic

Above: Ostrich chick at Chiredzi Wildlife Investments' game ranch where ostrich are reared alongside crocodile. Demand for both ostrich and crocodile leather is insatiable — and cholesterol-free, seven-kilo ostrich drumsticks are big sellers in America's health fad food markets.

Commission's regulations demand that exporting countries are free of foot-and-mouth disease. Wild bovines rapidly infect domestic stock.

To ensure control, many buffalo were killed and fences, vaccination zones and buffer zones were built around Hwange and Gonarezhou National Parks. In the long-term, however, ranching will damage the soil and grazing. Many experts believe that ultimately the land will have to be left to the buffalo — if any survive that long. Despite these precuations the ranching industry suffered a heavy outbreak of the disease in 1989 and lost its US$100 million a year European market.

Established as a National Park in 1975, Gonarezhou is mainly flat or undulating country, with scattered, isolated hills including the Chikunja Range, rising 2,000 feet above sea level, broken by the valleys of the Nuanetsi, Runde, and Save Rivers which abound with crocodile and many freshwater species, including turtle, lung fish, tigerfish, and bream. Amazingly, marine species of fish — tarpon and swordfish — have also been caught in the Runde, hundreds of kilometres from the saltwater of the Indian Ocean.

For almost half its journey through the park, the river's south bank is marked by the spectacular Chilojo Gorge, its red-sandstone cliffs riven by many gullies which the animals follow down to the water.

But the sanctuary's largest and most dominant feature is the Chipinda pools which form almost half the park and attract large numbers of migratory game from Kruger National Park in South Africa and a neighbouring game area in Mozambique.

Hundreds of eland and elephant regularly cross between Gonarezhou and Kruger. Resident species include black rhino and hippo. It is also a major stronghold for nyala, suni, and Lichtenstein's hartebeest. And, perhaps unique in Africa for so many different small antelope, colonies of steinbok, grysbok, grey duiker, Livingstone's suni, oribi, and klipspringer live close together.

For administration purposes the park has been divided into two sections: Chipinda Pools in the north and Mabalauta in the south. Only open during the May to October dry season, there are many campsites throughout the park and a comfortable rest camp at Chinguli in the centre. There are caravan sites at Chipinda Pools Camp and at Swimuwini Camp in the Mabalauta area. But to enter this part of the reserve you need written permission. Although game walks are allowed, visitors are cautioned to behave with discretion, particularly when close to elephant, buffalo, or rhino.

Much of the vegetation has suffered grievous harm from burning and bush clearing carried out during the tsetse control programme and by elephant. Dams and irrigation schemes have affected the flow and water quality of the Runde and Save rivers, and Manjinji Pan on the south bank of the Nuanetsi River, which used to be a haven for thousands of birds, is silting up.

Nonetheless Gonarezhou remains one of Zimbabwe's most pristine wildernesses. Magnificent to behold, memorable to experience, only one cloud darkens this natural Disneyland — the constant threat of poachers crossing the border from Mozambique.

6. Mountain and Moor, Forest and Waterfall

Sere and scorched, its arid floor cut by the wide reaches of the meandering Save River, the lowveld thrusts its spatula-shaped salient deep between the highveld and the wall of the eastern highlands, that massive buttress of granite mountains which form much of the country's border with Mozambique.

The Save, of all Zimbabwe's rivers second only in size to the mighty Zambezi, rises in the highveld some 100 kilometres south-west of Harare, then drops swiftly about 2,000 feet during the first 100 kilometres or so of its journey to the Indian Ocean, which it enters between Beira and Maputo. Its major tributary, the Runde, joins it at the Mozambique border. By the time it reaches the lowveld it has become sluggish.

Stunted patches of withered grass, rock, and sand characterize this unproductive land of almost perpetual famine. The only solace that the leached soil of the communal lands can offer to the people who attempt to eke a living from it is the flood bounty and dry season trickle of the Save. Theirs is the harshest of existences. Villagers walk long distances to collect their sacks of grain from the relief centres organized by the Government.

For those who only pass through it, however, the ravaged scenery holds a certain gaunt and barren beauty, especially when the first upthrust of the highland wall starts to shadow the eastern horizon some fifty kilometres out of Chiredzi.

That elusive shadow is the first manifestation of the cool and temperate substance to come: a delight of coffee and tea plantation, ancient forest and granite bluff, cloud-crested rocky peak and rolling moorland, and streams and glistening waterfalls scratched on 2,000 foot cliff faces.

From their southernmost point, 4,000-foot-high Mount Selinda — host to Chirinda Forest — the mountains stretch more than 300 kilometres to the massive granite bluffs of Nyanga National Park in the north.

The promise of Tanganda Junction, and the cool relief that lies beyond it, made when it is 100 kilometres distant, draws you through this haunting heat-ridden wilderness — bordered in the immediate east by Chipanga Safari Area where hunters stalk small and medium-sized antelope for their trophy room walls.

The large signs which renew the promise every forty kilometres suggest Tanganda Junction is an important centre. With only twenty kilometres to go, the road begins to climb a pass between two massive, forested whalebacks and there it is — a dream unfulfilled, no more than what the signposts say: a junction where two roads meet. There's not even a shack to justify the pledge.

But turn north and twenty-four kilometres of travel brings you to Birchenough Bridge, a small enough village with a large enough bridge to ensure its permanence. In 1935 it was the first of such size to be built of high tensile steel and the third longest bridge of its type in the world. It is named after Sir Henry Birchenough, President of the BSAC from 1925 to 1937.

Designed by Ralph Freeman of Sir Douglas Fox and partners of London, in all but size it is an exact replica of Sydney Harbour Bridge,

Opposite: Sunbright Tessa's Falls cascade down a rock face into a magic glen in the daunting Chimanimani mountains of Eastern Zimbabwe.

Previous pages: Tea plantation in the rolling hills around Chipinge at the southern end of the Chimanimani range. One of Zimbabwe's major export crops, it was first planted in this region in the 1920s.

Opposite: Rising 230 feet high, the single-span Birchenough Bridge named after a former President of the British South Africa Company was designed by Sir Ralph Freeman who, apart from the actual dimensions, faithfully copied his similar work for the world-famous Sydney Harbour Bridge. The 300 metre single span was widened and strengthened in 1984 to give it a new lease of life.

Australia, which he also designed. Indeed, from the Sydney bridge came the cable back stays that held the main arch ribs as they were placed in position. They were then deployed as the permanent hangars for the main deck structure.

Rising 230 feet, the ribs support a twenty-five-foot wide main span more than 1,000 feet long that hangs some sixty feet above the river. But even the broadest dreams outlive their reality and in 1984 the bridge's dimensions increased when it was widened and strengthened through a World Bank project.

Turn east at Tanganda Junction, however, and after thirty-seven kilometres of stiff, uphill travel, you arrive at delightfully sleepy Chipinge town, heart of the prettiest postcard countryside anyone could ever wish to see.

South of Chipinge on the slopes of Mount Selinda, the ten square kilometres of Chirinda Forest Botanical Reserve, 3,550 feet above sea level, protects an ancient legacy, one of Zimbabwe's few remaining primaeval rain forests. Rare and ancient indigenous red mahoganies shaft 200 feet through the tangled lianas to pierce the thick green canopy

Above: Forest plantations cover the foothills of the ancient Chimanimani mountains, the highest points forming an undulating ridge — seen in the background — which stretches almost 100 kilometres from north to south.

Left: The gardens of La Rochelle, former home of Sir Stephen and Lady Courtauld, now form a one-square-kilometre botanical garden filled with rare orchids and precious trees and shrubs just outside Mutare.

above the dappled, cathedral-like gloom of the forest glades.

Although the largest trees, there are only about 300 red mahogany in the forest. Most are concentrated in one locale known as the 'Valley of the Giants'. The oldest, which took root six centuries ago, rises 216 feet and is fifteen metres in circumference.

Other rare species include the ironwood, *Strychnos mitis*, not much used because it is difficult to work. The larger trees, which are often attacked by borers, suffer from dry rot. Another useful tree, Chitonga, *Strychnos mellodara*, is seldom more than 40 centimetres in diameter and rarely more than 100 feet high. Easily recognised by its dark green, leathery leaves, its tiny white flowers bloom in September and its yellow berries cover the forest floor in February. Although the hard, close-grained wood warps and cracks during drying, it is good for making cabinets.

This garden of nature is also noted for a rare blue ground orchid, *Callianthus natalensis*. More rare orchids and ferns add to the variety of its jungle undergrowth and the forest is rich in many other unique species of trees, plants and flowers.

Charles Francis Swynnerton, the naturalist who lived in the forest for two decades from the turn of the century, kept immaculate records and most of what is known of its flora, and fauna, stems from his impeccable observations.

Overleaf: Founded in 1896 flower-filled Mutare, cradled in a bowl of mountains, was the third town to bear the name Umtali.

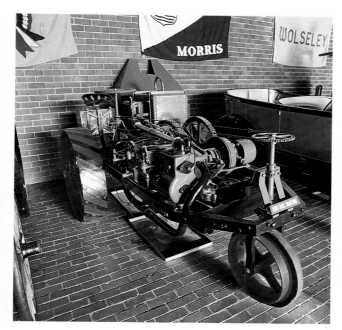

Above: Claimed to be the world's second-oldest tractor, this exhibit is the highlight of the transport display at the national museum in Mutare.

In 1892, the South African-based American Board Mission (later known as the 'East Central African Mission') set up a mission in twelve square kilometres of open forest land overlooking a fertile valley. The mission has prospered ever since. Its first church — with eighteen members — was formally established in 1897 with a second mission and day school at Chikore, thirty kilometres to the west.

Chipinge, complete with rustic pub and Tudor-style library, marks the southern extremity of the dramatic Chimanimani Mountains, here cast down into gentle, flowing hills; their contours moulded into unsurpassing beauty and their form fleshed with the emerald- and olive-green squares, oblongs, and rhomboids of tea and coffee estates.

These undulating slopes, rising and falling between 3,700 and 4,500 feet above sea level, are blessed with enough sun and rain to ensure that the quality of Zimbabwe's two major farm export commodities, after tobacco, command top prices on world markets. The first tea was planted in 1924 but it was another twenty-six years before coffee took root. Dairy farming also flourishes and Chipinge boasts three cheese factories.

Other major crops are pine, wattle, and macadamia nuts and in 1989 tobacco plantations were also beginning to burgeon in these fertile hills where the panorama changes round every bend in the road.

Between the plantations and forests, smallholdings of bananas and vegetables serve as lush contrast to the arid lowveld below. Here the hills, their slopes bathed in the gentle warmth of a late afternoon November sun, roll away to distant horizons.

This land took the breath of the first white man to reach them in the last decade of the last century. After weeks of slogging through the highveld and then the lowveld, Thomas Moodie strode up these hills in 1893, saw how good was the land, and strode no further. He had done more than enough to deserve his place in the sun but he paid the supreme price for his effort.

His nine-month trek from South Africa was a vital part of Rhodes's plan to occupy the eastern region for, despite the 1891 Anglo-Portuguese treaty which settled the borders of the disputed territories, the Portuguese still felt that Manicaland and Gazaland fell within their sphere of influence.

To establish a European settlement Rhodes commissioned George Benjamin Dunbar Moodie to recruit settlers from the Orange Free State — offering large farms in Gazaland to every man and boy who trekked there.

In turn, Dunbar Moodie invited his uncle, Thomas Moodie, a grain farmer in the Bethlehem district of the Free State, of Scottish descent from Melsetter in the Orkney islands, to lead the twenty-nine settler families, mostly Afrikaners — thirty-seven men and thirty-one women, with seventeen wagons and 350 horses and cattle — who set off in May, 1892.

Hit by foot-and-mouth disease, attacked by lion, and short of water, when the wagon train reached Fort Victoria most of the families quit and made their way northwards to Enkeldoorn and Salisbury.

Moodie set off on his second leg of his trek to an unknown land with only fourteen men, four women, three small children, and seven wagons. At the wide sandy reaches of the Save river, treacherous with quicksand, Moodie crossed the river from island to island on horseback marking out

a safe crossing for the wagons.

Then horse sickness attacked the horses and malaria the men. Soon after crossing the Save, the weakened party found their way barred by the massive granite barrier of Areman Hill. For more than a week they chopped, hewed, dug, and finally blasted their way through this forbidding gate — the route now followed by the main road from Birchenough Bridge to Masvingo — but could only get their wagons up the mountain by chaining three teams of oxen to each wagon. When they reached the top four days later they named the mountain 'Threespansberg'.

Finally, on 3, January, 1893, nine months after leaving Bethlehem, they reached the green rolling hills around Chipinge and halted by three clear waterfalls where Thomas Moodie claimed his own farm, naming it 'Waterfall'. He did not live long to enjoy his Eden. Although he saw the settlement he founded — Melsetter — pegged out, he was dead of blackwater fever within a year.

Ruined in health, having lost all she owned, Moodie's widow left the country in 1895. His nephew, Dunbar, fared no better. Given nine farms, he became a physical wreck trying to develop them. He was arrested for gun-running and died in 1897. He left no will and BSAC repossessed eight of the farms leaving his widow and children virtual paupers.

Thomas Moodie is remembered by the memorial that was raised in his honour on his Waterfall farm. It is marked as Moodie's Grave by the sign on the road from Tanganda Junction to Chimanimani, one of the earliest European settlements in Zimbabwe, and the village 'capital' of this stunningly beautiful mountain region.

The grave lies to the east of the road, at the point where it swoops down before climbing sharply upward to snake through a gorge cut from the solid cliff of the neighbouring Vumbere range, the western outliers of the Chimanimani region. The hairpin gorge blasted through the cliff by the highway engineers is gateway to what is arguably one of Africa's most dramatic and scenically lovely landscapes.

Though Zimbabwe's mountains claim no great heights, the view that greets you at the crest of the pass is proclamation enough of their magnificence, as much as the road is tribute to those who designed and built it.

The range forms a rampart that gathers the rain from the south-east monsoon winds sweeping inland from the Indian Ocean. Average rainfall in these parts varies between 1,000 and 1,270 millimetres a year.

No surprise, then, that the harvest these mountains yield is timber. Beneath peaks that rise as high as 6,400 feet, their slopes, both steep and precipitous, soft and gentle, are covered with thick cloaks of commercial plantations. The road twists and turns through the valleys as giant, exotic Australian eucalyptus sway in the wind.

Once blessed with an abundance of timber — from teak to mahogany — demand for fuelwood has had a rapacious effect on Zimbabwe's natural forests. Even trees held sacred by local communities now fall to the axe and the Government has launched a major conservation and reafforestation programme to halt the damage and restore the woodlands.

Above: Flowering aloe tree in the verdant beauty of Vumba Botanical Gardens.

Above: Rare plants abound in Vumba Botanical Gardens where a fountain plays in the middle of a lake beneath tree-shrouded slopes. The garden was bequeathed to the nation by its creator Fred Taylor. Covering two square kilometres in the Vumba mountains, the garden is a unique floral treasury.

Few trees provide as much wood as quickly as the fast-growing eucalyptus — gum tree — which forms the basis of the programme. But it has its critics. The tree draws too much water from the ground table and affects the hydrological balance. It also depletes the nutrients in the soil too quickly. Nor do its leaves and bark provide good fodder.

On the other hand, say eucalyptus supporters, no other tree can do more to stop the rape of the woodlands. And the tree gives other benefits; one species, *Eucalyptus mellodara*, is considered the best honey tree in the world and Zimbabwe's rapidly-growing honey industry is heavily dependent on the species. Other eucalyptus produce oils essential for pharmaceutical and industrial applications, and essences for perfumes.

But experiments with slower growing indigenous acacias also show promise and forestry experts believe their growth rate can be accelerated through selective breeding programmes.

One of these, the *Acacia albida*, thrives in alien habitats and loses its nitrogen-rich leaves at the start of summer when the soil is most in need. As a result livestock grow fat and glossy on its pods and leaves.

Above: White rhino in the Cecil Kop game sanctuary, Mutare.

Moreover, field crops can be grown right up to its trunk without affecting either.

Finally, climbing up through a dark grove of pine trees, the major forest plantation species, and other exotics, the road emerges at the aptly-named Skyline Junction overlooking Chimanimani Valley and the village that serves as capital of this region. The turn left drops down through the northern reaches of the Vumbere hills to Wengezi Junction on the lowveld salient. The right fork takes you into Chimanimani village and the heart of the mountains.

Moodie's Melsetter, where the tarmac ends, is a forestry and farming centre. Originally there were three Melsetters. South Melsetter became Chipinge in 1907 and the other was abandoned in 1930.

Chimanimani is the home of the Tshindao-speaking Vandao people, a widely-spoken language understood across a large area, from the lowlands of Mozambique as far north as Mutare. There are many ancient ruins similar in style but not scale to Great Zimbabwe and, more ancient still, bushmen rock paintings near the old drift, across the Save river.

The Chimanimani district covers 3,100 square kilometres. In the extreme south, at the junction of the Save and Runde rivers and no more than 1,000 feet above sea level, it is hot, humid, and uncomfortable. But Chimanimani, 152 kilometres from Mutare and 5,200 feet above sea level, is delightful contrast. This lovely village is the base from which to visit the scenic Bridal Veil Falls, Chimanimani National Park, Chimanimani Eland Sanctuary, and the many other attractions of this unspoilt region.

More than fifty kilometres across, the Chimanimani range stretches almost 100 kilometres from north to south in a grand array of peaks, the highest reaching 8,000 feet. It was formed when violent earth movements forced the quartzite massif against an immovable plateau and it folded over to create the dauntingly beautiful landscape you see today.

No roads enter this alpine zone although you can explore some of the foothills by four-wheel drive vehicle along rough tracks. Even on the scenic route to Cashel, skirting the midriff of 7,034-foot-high Musapi, the going is rugged.

The only way into the high mountains, however, is on foot along a single pathway, as ancient as the peaks themselves, that follows the old slave trail from the interior to the Indian Ocean coast.

The eastern boundary of the 171-square-kilometre national park, established in 1953, forms the border with Mozambique, and embraces all the major peaks, including the two highest points, 8,005-foot-high Binga and 7,267-foot-high Dombe. One major problem confronting the park's staff is the frequency at which forest and grass fires spread into the park from pastures and farmlands to threaten the forest. Because there are so few trails, they are extremely difficult to control.

Mutekeswane Camp, the park headquarters and gateway to the trail into the mountains, lies some twenty-five kilometres from Chimanimani village, along a gravel road at the base of the main range. It has a campsite but nothing else. Beyond this point you are on your own and it is no place for the comfort-seeker or the timid. Storms blow up in minutes and the mountains are frequently draped in impenetrable mist.

But mountain enthusiasts, walkers, hikers, and climbers, will revel in the sense of discovery and adventure that comes from exploring the steep, forest-clad slopes, ravines, and magic valleys that make this nature sanctuary such a delight. The major river born in the marsh sponge of this range is the Bundi.

Early morning finds the folds of the grasslands and the gaunt cliffs bathed in a soft, fine mist but soon the sun rises, flushing out the last clinging shadows lurking in the deepest rills. The white rocks sparkle with its fire and the promise of warmth to come and trout-filled streams, banked by a riot of colourful ferns and orchids, sweet peas and purple lassandria, and sensual pink creepers in choked abundance, chuckle their happiness at the pledge. One outstanding marshland species, the vivid red *Disa ornithantha*, flowers in January and February.

Fringing the moorlands that host these rare flowers and semi-tropical plants are the last remnants of the great native forests of giant cedars and yellow woods. Many plants are related to South Africa's south-western Cape region. Unusual, too, in Zimbabwe, the lower slopes of the mountains host some low-altitude rain forest.

Throughout, the flash of wild animals in startled flight — sable, eland, blue duiker, klipspringer — darting in and out of thicket and forest cover will delight the walker and climber who may also find an occasional leopard.

But the Chimanimani range is best known for its stunning birdlife, some of it unique in Zimbabwe, which includes violet-crested turaco, malachite sunbird, laughing dove, lark, visiting swifts and swallows, trumpeter hornbill, secretary bird, francolins, and many kinds of eagle.

Some distance south-east of Chimanimani village, Zimbabwe's

Above: Coffee plantation cloaks the slopes of the Vumba mountains with the bluff of Leopard Rock rising in the background.

Outward Bound Mountain School provides outdoor adventure training to shape young characters into independent and resourceful individuals. To the north of the village, the Bridal Veil Falls emerge from their forest shroud to cascade more than 150 feet down a series of steps in a delicate tracery almost like the silk that inspires their name.

Beyond the falls lie the 120 square kilometres of Chimanimani Eland Sanctuary established in 1975 with funds from the small Chimanimani community and the Conservation Trust of Zimbabwe.

Long present in Chimanimani's ancient forests, wild eland is the only species of all the large antelopes to have adopted the artificial habitat of the more recent pine plantations as its own. Indeed, they flourish in this supposedly unnatural environment. There are also some waterbuck and zebra.

On the winding scenic drive north through Tandai to Cashel, along a gravel trail, there are tantalizing glimpses of the Chimanimani's majestic peaks and occasional great panoramas over the Mozambique plains thousands of feet below.

At Cashel the tarmac resumes — leaving, in the distance ahead, remote and isolated, 7,255-foot-high Himalaya. The road heads west to Wengezi Junction on the lowveld where you join the main road that takes you sixty-seven kilometres to Mutare, once known as Umtali, capital of Manicaland, and the most fertile and scenic region in Zimbabwe.

Mutare is an international city. The Mozambique border is marked by a chainmesh fence, wasteland, and floodlights in one of the urban areas closest to the city centre. It is also the terminal of the oil pipeline from Beira which discharges its products at Feruka, a few kilometres west of the city.

Farming and mining are the mainstays of the city economy although

Opposite: Sunlight and shadow play against each other in a eucalyptus plantation on the Vumba Mountains.

Above: Honde Valley tea picker.

the manufacturing section has developed rapidly recently and now includes a vehicle assembly plant, glass, timber, paper, textile, and food processing industries. Even so, nothing in its rapidly-expanding industrial area can diminish Mutare's glory.

Encircled by graceful hills and mountains, its wide and pleasant streets are ablaze with colour all year round. The superb civic centre surrounded by manicured lawns and flowerbeds is the city centrepiece, its modern theatre and concert hall the legacy of Sir Stephen and Lady Courtauld whose old home, 'La Rochelle', some way outside the city, is now a botanical garden displaying rare orchids and precious trees and shrubs. The city's museum matches that of Bulawayo for the quality of its exhibits, though different in style and presentation.

As cities go, it suffers no overcrowding (indeed, it is said that Mutare is most suited to the newly-wed or newly-dead). In terms of population — far outranked by Bulawayo, Gweru, and Chitungiwiza, Harare's satellite — it is a minnow of scarcely 150,000 people. But even if fifth in head count, it claims to be third in importance. Mutare has always prided itself on its place in national history.

The original settlement was built seventeen kilometres from the present city at the place where the powerful Manica chief, Mutasa, whose favours and support were courted by both the British and the Portuguese, built his kraal. It was here, in 1888, that some prospectors approached Mutasa for permission to search for gold in the Penhalonga valley, cut by the river Mutare, named after the Chimanyika word for metal.

Soon after, A. R. Colquhoun led an advance party of the Pioneer Column to the kraal where they built a fort — ostensibly to protect the chief from the Portuguese, strategically to establish a stranglehold on

Opposite: Combined large-scale tea and coffee plantation in eastern Zimbabwe along the Mozambique border. The combination of sun and rain in equal amounts sustains the high-grade quality of both crops. Tea is a bush and coffee a tree and their roots hold the soil and rainfall and guard against erosion.

Mutasa and the Manica people — which became the first Umtali. It was manned by a police contingent under Captain H. M. Heyman. They were soon followed by the first settlers who made camp near the confluence of the Mutare and Sambi rivers.

But the settlement did not last long. Driven by gold fever, prospectors staked claims everywhere, even in the fort, and then proceeded to undercut the entire area until it was a treacherous honeycomb. Abandoned in 1891, a second township was established near the Mutare river. The ruins of that old fort still stand, testimony to Rhodes's imperial obsession and the lust for wealth which drove the 'pioneers'.

The new township flourished. From 1893 it was administered by a sanitary board governed by a committee of six under the Civil Commissioner. By March, 1895, it had a population of almost 100; seventy-eight men, thirteen women, and nine children, with a crude hospital, post office, bakery, butchery, church, and cemetery.

It was indeed a promising prospect. Directly on the border with Portuguese-ruled Mozambique, Umtali assumed strategic importance as the proposed headquarters of the railway from Beira on the Indian Ocean that would drive through to Fort Salisbury and on to Bulawayo to link up with the line from South Africa. It would then move north to complete the Cape to Cairo link that Rhodes planned as part of the British conquest of Africa.

The railway arose from the 1891 Anglo-Portuguese treaty, after which the BSAC formed the Beira Railway Company. Contractor George Pauling began construction at Fontesvilla in September, 1892. For more than five years his labour force of about 1,200 men struggled through the tsetse-fly infested scrub of lowland Mozambique, battling not only heat but fatal malaria, blackwater fever, and sleeping sickness.

Above: Dramatic Pungwe Falls drop more than 800 feet off the rolling Nyanga Downs into the Pungwe Gorge before descending another 4,000 feet down the escarpment wall into the Honde Valley below.

Above: Wattle and pine plantations flourish around the borders of Nyanga National Park.

The narrow-gauge line, following the course of the Menini river valley from Macaque, reached the place where Mutare now stands on 4 February, 1898. And faced an insurmountable barrier — the daunting climb over Christmas Pass (named by the army engineer assigned to build a road over it after he made camp there on Christmas Day 1891). The incline was too steep, nor was a tunnel feasible.

Pauling suggested to Rhodes that Umtali, by now a flourishing gold rush town with four hotels, one weekly newspaper, the handset *Umtali Advertiser*, library, two banks, and the trading store established by Thomas Meikle and his brothers, would have to be moved a second time.

Promising compensation totalling around $100,000 to all those who agreed to move, Rhodes organised the transfer under a government notice of 1 October, 1896. Many wood and iron buildings from the old town were carried over Christmas Pass and laid out on the farms established by three of the original settlers, Sable Valley, Waterfall Mountain View, and Berkeley. In plan it was exactly like the second settlement, each owner occupying roughly the same site.

The Sanitary Board held its last meeting in 'old' Umtali on 11 August, 1887, and its first in the 'new' Umtali on 29 September. The BSAC built a $6,000 dam for town water. Here the railway established its headquarters and the loco workshops that served the entire system for many years. 'Old Umtali' was left to the missionaries of the American Methodist Church (the mission and training school they built were still functioning in 1989).

Development was swift. In 1899 the town fathers built a tramway, the only one ever to operate in Zimbabwe, between the railway station and the town centre by way of Main Street. It was maintained by

railway engineers who also carried out much work in the neighbouring mines and farms.

Six months after the inauguration of the Salisbury-Umtali line, the original narrow-gauge track was replaced on 1 August, 1900, with a standard gauge line and the Beira Railway company amalgamated with the Mashonaland Railway Company.

In 1910 the wood and iron railway headquarters were dismantled, loaded on to special trucks, and taken to Bulawayo. But the workshops maintained the Garrett steam locomotives for many years afterwards and, much later, assumed responsibility for major overhauls of the diesel-electric fleet.

Mutare became a municipality in June, 1914, and a city on 1, October, 1971, when the war for independence was being fought and the army took over the Cecil Hotel — remembered for its large verandah, tastefully furnished lounge and writing rooms, and long airy corridors. The modern Manica Hotel, operated by Zimbabwe Sun, was completed on the neighbouring plot in 1974.

Mutare still depends on farming and mining for much of its prosperity and the yearly Agricultural and Horticultural Society Show, first staged in 1900, draws thousands of visitors from all over the country.

Above Christmas Pass, from the 5,000-foot-high crest of Umtali Heights, just beneath Cecil Kop, reached by a snaking hairpin road with precipitous drops on either side, orange spears shaft northward through the lowering clouds of sundown to pierce gold-rich

Above: Rocky crest of Zimbabwe's highest mountain, 8,504-foot-high Inyangani.

Above: Cussonia spicata, *one of the lovely trees endemic to the southern Cape region, flourishes in the heights of Nyanga National Park.*

Penhalonga Valley along the Mozambique border. Down below to the south, where the street lights twinkle, night has already fallen over slumbering Mutare sheltered in its mountain cradle.

At the base of the ridge, a viewpoint also overlooks either side of Christmas Pass. It was here in the 1950s that Britain's Queen Elizabeth, the Queen Mother, unveiled a monument raised to Kingsley Fairbridge, an ardent South African-born advocate of white settlement in the British Empire. So much so that he organized the migration of thousands of British orphans and unwanted children to Canada, Australia, and what was then Rhodesia, in a scheme that, in 1988, became the subject of a critical British television documentary investigation.

After Independence, the monument was removed. It is now on view in the National Museum settler house in Mutare's Fourteenth Avenue where Harry Went, a scion of one of the original pioneers, was born. It was the third house to be built in Mutare and only a street away the first house built in the new town, Three Steps, is still a fashionable city residence, as are many of Mutare's original buildings.

In the main museum, in Victory Avenue, the Transport Gallery has an outstanding number of exhibits including what must be the Dorchester of London's Edwardian telephone kiosks, large enough to be a bed-sit, and horse-drawn carriages, vintage cars, and early locomotives. The Boultbee Gallery, named after the first curator, Captain E. F. Boultbee, OBE, contains a range of armour and smallarms covering more than 500 years.

Most, however, will find the natural history displays the most compelling. You can open a hatch and study a live bee colony at work in its hive, or walk through a door onto a balcony in an outdoor aviary that contains almost 600 birds representing more than fifty species from four major families. Other displays in this superb museum focus on cultures and landscapes.

Two roads lead east from Mutare: one down to the Mozambique border post and, beyond that, the village of Machipanda; the other upwards on the long winding road that climbs more than 2,000 feet in eighteen kilometres into the 'Mountains of Mist', those tree-shrouded bastions that guard the city's south-east flanks.

The view north over the city on the first section could hardly be equalled — until it disappears around the next hairpin and you find the unfolding panorama of the 'Mountains of Mist' as they roll away, each ridge ascending higher, to the east, south-east, and south.

Just beyond this point, at the Prince of Wales Viewpoint, with a drop of several hundred feet beneath, you can take in, far below, Machipanda and the Beira Corridor of Mozambique. High above to the south-east are the olive-green slopes of the Vumba Mountains. Their highest point is no more than 6,300 feet, but every foot, from the majestic forested crests that drop down to flanks scored by deep-cut valleys, proclaims their alpine status.

The road leads on to magic valleys. One in the east hides many palatial houses on its slopes, and the rustic White Horse Inn whose architecture and service bespeak an impeccable pedigree. At 5,200 feet you come to Cloudlands, the junction between the scenic route around these marvellous mountains and the road to Vumba Botanical Garden and Bunga Forest Botanical Reserve.

Casting their shade on either side of the road, the fifteen-square-kilometre reserve's sturdy indigenous trees are nourished by the abundant rain trapped by the 'Mountains of Mist'. Rambling, well-kept footpaths guide the visitor through the dappled shadows of this thick and luxuriant unspoilt forest wonderland. It deserves a day's outing and more.

The botanical garden is the gift of Fred Taylor, a settler from the north of England, who so delighted in the splendour of his adopted home that he moulded two square kilometres of forest into a landscaped garden of sublime proportions which he named, prosaically, Manchester Park.

Now a national park, here man and nature combined to create enduring beauty. Motes of sun strike through the forest canopy and glisten in the streams. Fish flicker in the crystal clear ponds and lakes. Moss and ferns cling to the stone footpaths of the humid forest groves. Fuchsias, hydrangeas, azaleas, begonias, lilies, protea, cycads, orchids, and aloes paint the verdant lawns and forest glades in brilliant colours. Many of the trees and shrubs can be found nowhere else in Zimbabwe. Rising 6,000 feet at its highest point, the garden also offers a resplendent panorama of the Mozambique plain more than 3,000 feet below.

But Vumba is not just a repository of floral and botanical glory. The surrounding botanical reserve is rich in wildlife as ornithological and botanical studies at the splendidly-named Seldomseen Naturalist Centre have revealed.

Here graceful antelope — blue duiker and bushbuck — bushpig, baboon, and Samango monkey haunt the glades, cliffs, and forest. And soaring in the thermals above the cliffs, darting through the upper storeys of the forest, or flitting on the forest floor is an outstanding display of birds including the orange ground thrush, wood owl, red-winged starling, bronze sunbird, augur buzzard, forest weaver, Nyasa crimson-wing, Swynnerton's robin, and two species endemic to Zimbabwe, *Chirinda apalis* and Roberts' *prinia*.

The gardens lie in the eastern lee of 6,270-foot-high Castle Beacon and from the gate the road hairpins south beneath the magnificent rock bluff of Leopard Rock to reveal a manicured landscape of rolling coffee plantations and, in the hazy distance far beneath, the waters of Mozambique's Chicamba Real, a large and impressive manmade lake.

In 1989 workmen were preparing to refurbish Leopard Rock Hotel, a fair imitation of the Palace of Versailles, that sits beneath the southern face of the bluff. The granite crest, once the haunt of leopard, is known to the local communities as Chinyakwaremba — the 'hill that sat down'. Their folklore tells how the spirits were angered by the villagers that lived at its base and so caused the mountain to fall upon them.

Seymour Smith built the hotel after the Second World War and it was given the royal accolade in the 1950s when Queen Elizabeth, the Queen Mother, and Princess Margaret stayed there. But after liberation forces attacked it in the 1970s it was closed down.

From Cloudlands the circular scenic route switchbacks beneath the heights of 6,139-foot-high Lion Rock up and down through cool, lofty eucalyptus forests, and into neat coffee plantations.

Opposite: Mysterious ruins of Nyangwe Fort in Nyanga National Park continue to pose riddles for archaeologists.

Four centuries ago, after a long trek west under Chief Zimunya, the Mbire people arrived at these mountains and found them welcoming. The forests and caves were a natural fortress against marauding enemies and animals and they reinforced them with their own defences. You can still see the ruins.

Gravel road for much of the way, the route snakes down along the Mozambique border to rejoin the tarmac in the scorching heat of Burma Valley where tea, tobacco, and banana plantations thrive.

Finally, it cuts through the Zimunya communal lands and Chitakatira town and back to the Prince of Wales viewpoint where mesmerised but scheduled tourists must, sadly, take their last fill of these magnificent hills and return to Mutare for the next leg of their *Journey through Zimbabwe*.

Early next morning mist boils and billows over the top of 5,700-foot-high Cecil Kop as you follow the road out of Mutare over Christmas Pass towards Harare. Soon you turn north through Mutasa communal lands, past the mission town of old Umtali, to the most impressive of all Zimbabwe's eastern reaches.

Beyond old Umtali, two massive granite bluffs, the black, swollen bellies of the midmorning rain clouds nudging their brows, guard the approach to Nyanga. Some distance beyond these a road turns east through thick pine plantations to the edge of a majestic escarpment.

Below, tin roofs glinting in the sun, lie the farms and settlements of the communal lands of the Honde Valley. Skirting each contour of the almost sheer escarpment hanging above it in the west, the precipitous road now drops 4,500 feet into the valley in no more than thirty kilometres.

Waterfalls weep down the escarpment's massive dark and sombre face — ribbons of white lace on a black granite shroud — with the hills and plains of Mozambique stretching away into azure infinity on the eastern horizon.

Five thousand feet beneath the crown of Zimbabwe's highest summit, 8,504-foot-high Inyangani, the valley's northern reaches are marked by what arguably are among the loveliest plantation landscapes in the world. In their cultivation, tea and coffee are two crops that grace the countryside with an especial beauty and here, growing side by side upon one rolling hill after the other, they clothe the Honde Valley with a mantle of arborescent perfection.

The bright early afternoon sun gives way to brooding and distended rain clouds. Thunder echoes around the hills and lightning cleaves the sky. Sudden torrential downpours flood the roads, steam rises and tendrils of mist drift over the plantations, caressing the emerald crown of the tea bushes and the dark verdure of the coffee trees.

The road comes to an end in the tea-clad hills of the Aberfoyle Plantation. The only way out is to backtrack the ninety kilometres along the valley and up the escarpment to a winding gravel road, rising and falling through great pine and wattle plantations, that skirts the edge of the Nyanga escarpment.

It leads to the threshold of Nyanga National Park — a land of mountain and moor, forest and waterfall. Most of the park's 330 square kilometres, standing on a giant plateau of uplifted doleritic intrusions

Above: The delicate pastel bloom of a lily flower indigenous to Nyanga National Park.

Above: Colourful protea, a plant indigenous to the slopes of Mount Inyangani.

over granite, lies between 6,500 and 7,500 feet above sea level rising to the summit of Inyangani.

These highlands have been a favourite holiday retreat for most of this century. Rhodes paid his first to Nyanga in 1897 when he travelled by coach from Umtali. He was so taken by the beauty of the area that he established an estate of eighty-two square kilometres.

To stock it, he imported cattle herds from Mozambique and started experimenting with fruit growing. The first apples on his estate were cultivated by Dunbar Moodie, then his farm manager. Fruit growing has become a thriving industry (there is a fruit research station near Nyanga) and, bequeathed to the nation, the Rhodes estate now forms part of the national park.

Earlier cultures also found it safe and pleasant. Stone ruins established by an agricultural people of remarkable technical sophistication, dating back many centuries, cover hundreds of square kilometres. They built irrigation channels, fed by the mountain streams and planted their crops in terraced fields. Their outlines are still clearly visible on the mountain slopes. And across the slopes of Inyangani are the ruins of a chain of forts of remarkable complexity.

Rich in forests and rolling downs, many important rivers — Pungwe, Odzi, Gairezi, Nyangombe, and Mtarazi — are born in the park to tumble over the escarpment in a series of magnificent waterfalls, including the 2,500-foot Mtarazi Falls which plunge sheer into the Honde Valley.

The indigenous vegetation, including a stand of Malange cedar, the country's only native conifer, stunted woodlands, patches of lowland forest, and high altitude heathlands, has strong affinities with South Africa's southern Cape Province.

Though there are relatively few animals, Nyanga is an important mountain wildlife and bird sanctuary with a range of species unique in Zimbabwe. On the mountain downs nyala and duiker drift like phantoms through the clouds that frequently roll across them. Cisticolas, waxbills, mannikins, widow-birds, buzzards, and eagles, all flourish in these heady heights.

But the rapid disappearance of the natural forest outside the park, and frequent fires, threatens many of the birds and the animals that migrate seasonally between them and the park.

Essentially scenic, the area inspires a range of outdoor recreational activities including quality angling for introduced rainbow, brown, and brook trout. Many rivers have been dammed to form small lakes and, stocked with trout, provide a challenge for the holiday fly-fisherman during a season extending from October to April. Visitors can also enjoy golf, tennis, and boating.

Well served by hotels, caravan parks, and campsites, the pleasantly rustic but modern capital of the region, just outside the northern perimeter of the park, is Nyanga, 6,162 feet above sea level (the name derives from 'Inyanga', the place of the witchdoctors).

Standing several hundred feet above it to the north-east is the alpine resort of Troutbeck, established in 1951 by Colonel A. H. MacIlwaine. Another resort, Juliasdale, lies some twenty-four kilometres south of Nyanga on the Rusape road that cuts through the Inyanga downs.

Off the southern dirt road through the misty forest a single-lane track leads east to a small glade with a picnic bench that is at the heart of the Nyanga's neighbouring Mtarazi Falls National Park.

A small footpath leads out of the glade onto the rock-strewn approach to the escarpment's edge, down to the Mtarazi River and a precarious foothold just above the point where the waters disappear over the lip of the sheer, 2,500-foot drop into the Honde Valley and lizards scuttle over the granite rocks. Late afternoon sunlight strikes through the billowing clouds like a celestial ray to stalk the shadows where the river falls.

Some kilometres beyond this spot, just off the main dirt road, another turn invites you again to the giddying edge of the escarpment where the brave can stand on a solitary granite rock 5,000 feet above the Honde Valley and gaze upon its sun-dappled beauty.

Now you enter Nyanga National Park and follow the winding road to Pungwe Falls viewpoint, not at the escarpment's edge, but far below where the downs roll away from the long spine of the high peaks and it drops 800 feet into the deep gorge of the Pungwe valley. There it winds

Above: Beautiful Nyangombe Falls, a popular tourist attraction in Nyanga National Park.

eastwards to take a final leap 4,000 feet down the escarpment where, levelled out, it flows lazily on towards the Indian Ocean.

From the viewpoint the moorland road switchbacks up and down valleys, past ancient ruins whose purpose still defies the archaeologists, to Mare Dam, a manmade resort that reflects the tranquillity of nature. Neat lodges welcome the visitor as does the trout hatchery and research centre which rears millions of fish to stock Nyanga's dams and rivers throughout the fishing season.

Brood stock, which mature at two years, are chosen for their high yield, rapid growth rates, body conformation, coloration, and disease resistance. Breeding takes place during the winter months of June, July, and August. Males are kept upstream because the female hormones induces fighting that causes excessive injuries.

Three months before spawning, the fish are placed on a diet of specially-formulated pellets containing Carophyll Red, used to give colour to a popular brand of orange soda, which — besides quenching human thirsts — improves the production and fertility of trout eggs.

Since each female is only ripe for about three days of the year they are checked twice a week. When ready the females are taken into the hatchery building together with the males. Stripping is carried out under artificial light. Ultraviolet sunlight, which under natural conditions is shielded by water and the nest, damages or destroy eggs .

Fertilization is almost immediate. Expansion, which starts when the eggs come into contact with water, lasts about twenty minutes. To initiate the expansion and harden the shells, a little water is added to the bowls.

Later, the fertilized eggs are washed two or three times to remove excess milt and debris, measured, and placed in the incubation trays.

Initial development of the embryo takes place between forty-eight and seventy-two hours after stripping. Depending on water temperatures, the eyed stage — when two little black dots, the embryo's eyes, can be seen through the egg shell — is reached between eight and nine days later.

Now the eggs are siphoned out and swirled around in a plastic bucket, a shock treatment guaranteed to kill any eggs which have not developed and so avoid infection of the healthy eggs. The eggs take between three and five weeks to hatch, depending on water temperatures.

After the fry have absorbed the yolk sac and reached the 'swim up' stage, they are taken to the raceways where, initially, they are fed on daphnia pellet powder and minced meat and lungs mixed with gelatin. Daphnia, water fleas, are bred in special ponds.

Trout have variable growth rates. To ensure uniformity of size, fry and fingerlings are graded frequently in a rectangular box with spaced, parallel bars along its base. Small fish slip between the bars separating them from the larger fish.

Fingerlings are reared in circular ponds until they are more than twenty centimetres long. To protect them from the hammerkop and the giant kingfisher, two major predators in Nyanga, the ponds are covered with wiremesh. Another savage predator, active during winter months, is the clawless otter.

Unprotected, these unwary fish are easy prey for the raider. Shadows on the breeding ponds turn the waters into a raging maelstrom as the trout, with Pavlovian reflex, swarm in avaricious schools ready for the first scattering of food.

Trout depend on high oxygen levels. Aeration increases the dissolved oxygen content in water — and aerated ponds can hold double their normal capacity. During the long hot summer months, when Nyanga trout often suffer from bacterial infection, this aeration helps reduce stress. Heat makes them miserable and sluggish. The best fishing is when the rains are plentiful, the temperature low, and the trout are lively and eager to take the fly.

The dam lies beneath the heights commanded by the ruins of Fort Nyangwe, one of a chain that lead across the lower slopes of Inyangani. But of all the ruins in this region the most stupendous, and baffling, are those discovered by van Niekerk in 1905 — spread across eighty square kilometres on the extreme northern edge of the Nyanga mountains.

The turn east from the dam, however, takes you to the base of the most popular climb up dramatic Inyangani, the road winding along ridges which look down into deep valleys where nyala stand frozen in the moment of discovery. Though of no great height, sudden storms and mist endow Inyangani with its own latent menace. Many have been lost and died on its high slopes.

Not far from Mare Dam are the park headquarters with the pretty little lake formed by the Rhodes dam (overgrown tees indicate its shores were once a golf course) overlooked by the Rhodes Nyanga Hotel, a throwback to the days of genteel colonial glory, which *Time* magazine's John Borrell described in a January, 1990, essay on Zimbabwe ten years after Independence.

He ate a six course meal in the dining room of Rhodes's former Nyanga farmhouse, served in such style by the hotel's blue-liveried retainers that he concluded the old rascal, whose portrait still gazes down upon diners, would have approved. The nearby stables have been converted by the Zimbabwe National Trust into a museum filled with memorabilia of the great imperialist and the region.

There's an undeniable peace to be found in the hotel's immaculate gardens and everywhere you travel in this region — whether it be the enchanting Nyangombe Falls, meaning 'where the cattle may be heard', near the Udu Dam, or the heady heights of Troutbeck, once a place of spectacular open moorland.

It was transformed in the late 1940s and 1950s by the energies of one man into a leisure and retirement resort without equal where thick forest and landscaped golf course now counterpose the undulating downs.

Colonel MacIlwaine, who probably did more than anyone to promote trout fishing at Nyanga, and was certainly the greatest fly fisherman in Zimbabwe, was the mastermind behind the Troutbeck estate at the centre of which is arguably Zimbabwe's most exclusive hotel.

Graciously luxurious, yet always rustic, the Troutbeck Hotel which boasts its own sparkling trout-filled lake and superb nine-hole golf course, has given birth to a tiny English-style village complete with bakery.

Above: Holidaymakers in search of sport on the waters of Troutbeck close to Nyanga National Park.

Many people have built retirement homes in the forest directly above the hotel, overlooking the three delightful little Connemara tarns, frequently shrouded in mist, created by Colonel MacIlwaine. The estate ends in the daunting north-western escarpment of the Nyanga mountains.

On a clear day, thousands of feet above the surrounding plains, you can look out from the aptly-named 'World's View, 7,086 feet above sea level, over the infinity of Zimbabwe's middleveld.

A stone monument indicates the direction of major centres and their distance, including Harare, directly north-west more than 200 kilometres away. So vast is the panorama, however, it's easy enough to imagine that the faint smudge on the lip of the far horizon could be the capital itself.

Col MacIlwaine, who died in 1983 aged ninety-four and whose 'vision and achievement created Troutbeck and Connemara', is buried in the grounds of the quaint interdenominational chapel of St. Catherine's on the downs just a few kilometres east of Troutbeck. It has no resident preacher but serves faithfully the community that so

Opposite: One of the three Connemara lakes fashioned at the inspiration of Colonel A. H. MacIlwaine.

evidently faithfully serves it. Both chapel and graveyard are immaculately-maintained.

MacIlwaine's contemporary, ninety-one-year-old Charles Gordon Hanmer, who died two years later, and 'whose valiant spirit built roads and planted trees opening Inyanga Downs to all who entered', is another laid to rest among the dozen or so graves in the tiny graveyard which also includes that of eighteen-year-old Second Lieutenant John Charles Innes, killed in action on 29 October, 1978.

The lives and achievements of the two ancients testify to the hopes which inspired all those settlers who found their way to Rhodesia in the early part of the century, dreaming perhaps that here they would build another, more idyllic 'sceptre'd isle'. At any rate, they found in these dramatic and rugged, but nonetheless tranquil heights, something of the cold beauty of their own native moorlands and hills — while the grave of gallant young Innes speaks tragically of the futility of those dreams.

7. Lakeland, the Gift of the Zambezi

Strange footsteps, imprinted in the sands of time and now laid bare in the fossil sands of the Zambezi Valley, reveal that a curious species of dinosaur — meat-eating, reptilian giants that walked on two legs — roamed this region more than 150 million years ago.

No doubt many more prehistoric secrets have been drowned by the deep waters of the manmade lake that covers 5,000 square kilometres of the middle Zambezi Valley between Victoria Falls and Kariba Gorge.

Why the dinosaurs suddenly vanished from the face of earth remains a mystery. But it is clear that some unexpected, natural catastrophe caused their extinction.

Only the latecomer, mankind, has found the ability to transform the environment and landscape on a scale that sometimes matches that of nature's forces — both in perspective and catastrophe. Though awesome to all those who behold it close up, the Kariba dam seems all too puny for the task of containing one of the world's largest inland seas.

Indeed, when you stand on the slender crest of the dam, the mind struggles to comprehend what it has achieved — an irrevocable change not just in the shape and character of the Zambezi Valley but of the Zimbabwe nation.

Kariba is 366 kilometres from Harare, and the Otto Beit Bridge at Chirundu, the border post downstream from Kariba between Zimbabwe and Zambia, is 355 kilometres from the capital. The road cuts over the mineral-rich Great Dyke and through the productive farmlands and goldfields of the highveld.

Place names along the way, Alaska and Eldorado among them, ring with the romance of those gold rushes that captured the imaginations of the nineteenth century. Alaska and Eldorado lie 115 kilometres from Harare on either side of Chinhoyi, headquarters of the Lomagundi district named after Chief Lomagundi who died from a Ndebele spear after refusing to pay Lobengula tribute.

Eldorado, in fact, is a misnomer: this was no city of treasure, just proof that all that glisters is not gold. It has disappointed countless people from the day that a hunter, following an antelope he had wounded but not killed, stumbled on the ancient gold workings. The hunter, A. Eyre, staked a claim but sold out to two prospectors who found the seam unprofitable.

Nonetheless, in 1904, after the discovery of a possible gold formation that might be of the same size and value as that on the Witwatersrand in South Africa, one astute share pusher used the lure of its name, from that fabled city of gold in Latin America, El Dorado, as the bait to make a fortune.

Although the find was untried, he proceeded to peg claims along several kilometres of the 'gold reef' and word of this new find soon spread. The operator then manipulated the share market and a new gold rush began. Hundreds of gullible treasure hunters from South Africa and Europe flocked to buy his claims, only to find their stake worthless.

In recent years copper mining at nearby Alaska and Mangula have contributed to the prosperity of Chinhoyi. Copper, in fact, has been

worked in this area for centuries. Copper crosses, used long ago as currency, are still unearthed occasionally by farmers.

But Chinhoyi's fame rests on an outstanding natural feature, eight kilometres north of the town; a perpendicular, thirty-metre-wide, 150-foot-deep limestone shaft, joined by several passages and caves, at the bottom of which lies a large pool of clear water 300 feet deep. The labyrinth for long served as refuge for local people from raiding warriors.

It was 'discovered' by the hunter Frederick Courtney Selous who, in May 1888, gave a dissertation on the subject to the Royal Geographical Society in London. The caves and pool form one of those rare places where reality actually exceeds travel brochure hyperbole.

Climbing down the steep granite steps it is easy enough to imagine you are approaching the entrance to Hades and the river Styx. All light vanishes. The silence is both eerie and profound, the dimensions gargantuan and vertiginous.

And then, at a twist in the tunnel, the revelation: there at the bottom it stands, limpid and translucent, a fathomless pool of deepest blue. If

Above: Chinhoyi Cave, 150 feet deep, where a pool of flawlessly-clear blue water fills another 300 feet of this fascinating, natural limestone shaft. The cave, linked by a number of subterranean passages, was 'discovered' by Frederick Courtney Selous, the celebrated nineteenth-century elephant hunter.

Above: Male bushbuck in Mana Pools National Park, a rare World Heritage Site.

you are lucky enough to catch it when the midmorning sun is directly above the water it sparkles with the hidden fires of a priceless turquoise.

And there's another formidable hole in the ground, sixteen kilometres west of Chinhoyi, on the Copper Queen road, at the site of the largest and most impressive ancient mine workings in the country. These are marked by the large slabs of monolithic rock removed from the depths by those miners of old when they gouged out a hole that measures half a kilometre long, 150 metres wide, and eighty feet deep.

Karoi, eighty kilometres north-west of the caves, announces itself with a signpost depicting a witch riding a broom. You may wonder why this is the town emblem and why, unlike all the other towns of Zimbabwe, there's no word of welcome or farewell. Is unwelcoming Karoi bewitched or bewitching? In fact, Karoi's name derives from the Bantu word *Karoyi*, little witch. Long ago it was the practice in these parts to throw witches into the river.

Now one of the greatest tobacco growing areas in Zimbabwe, for more than half a century Karoi was regarded as unsuitable for human

Right: Zambezi Valley fish eagle, whose haunting call echoes over the riverine forests, carries a newly-caught tigerfish back to its perch.

settlement (those witches perhaps?). Not until Robbie Robertson established Buffalo Downs farm in 1938 — after protracted arguments with civil servants who considered the tsetse-fly infested scrub too unhealthy — was the spell broken.

Robertson's first tobacco crop in 1939, planted on 100 acres, produced more than 1,100 kilos an hectare — double the normal yield — and its quality was so high that it sold at almost thirty per cent more than the top price, provoking a Parliamentary debate.

At once farmers began to clamour for land around Karoi then known as Urungwe. Its real development, however, only began after the Second World War. The name changed to Karoi soon after and the approaches to the town, with its well-planned and cared for landscaped gardens and smart streets reflects its prosperity and efficiency.

Eighty-seven kilometres after leaving this town that wishes neither welcome nor goodbye you arrive at Makuti. Here a road west leads to Kariba, while the main road runs straight on to Chirundu where the swift-flowing Zambezi River funnels through a 370-metre-wide gorge.

Until 1939 the only way you could cross the river was by pontoon and before that by dugout canoe upstream against the main current and then aimed, with furious strokes, at the distant landing stage.

For centuries the Zambezi has attracted adventurers. The people who come to explore it today by canoe, by vehicle, and on foot also discover its excitement — and its sense of timelessness. The most frequented stretch of water for these safaris is the 256 kilometres downstream from Kariba, under the Otto Beit Bridge at Chirundu, to

Kanyemba on the Mozambique border, which was a busy trading post in the seventeenth century. Portuguese merchants followed the river's course this far into the interior.

Designed by Sir Ralph Freeman of Sydney and Birchenough Bridge fame, the 415-metre bridge that now spans the gorge was built just before the Second World War. It was funded by the Beit Trust and named after Alfred Beit's brother, Sir Otto Beit, whose widow, Lady Lilian, opened it on 24 May, 1939. It remains the fastest land link between Harare and the Zambian capital of Lusaka which is 125 kilometres beyond the border.

The Otto Beit Bridge symbolizes the ever increasing threat facing the wild and wonderful Zambezi as the world of man pushes closer and closer. The Zambezi Valley's fossil records tell of the many dramatic changes which have taken place. Prised from the windblown sands, ashes, and rocks of the valley's steep gorges, abrupt escarpments, and gentle plains, these narrate epic stories of glacial activity, earth movements, and climatic disturbance.

They tell of times when the valley had abundant water and was covered with temperate forest, of other times when it was nothing but a desert, and of the massive lava flows that flowed through it. The sands preserved the footprints — forty centimetres from heel to toe — of a dinosaur that walked on two legs in this region 150 million years ago.

In modern times, the most profound change has been caused by the Kariba dam, particularly in this downstream stretch of the middle Zambezi Valley where the now fairly constant all year round water flow has had a profound and, sometimes, disturbing effect on river life.

Until the 1980s the floodgates were opened frequently and the artificial but sediment-free floods caused extensive erosion. Large amounts of fertile, alluvial soil were washed away and some fish species which used to breed under the cover of flooded vegetation, where the young were relatively safe from predation, faced extinction.

In twenty years, one thirty-kilometre-stretch between Mana Pools and the confluence of the seasonal Sapi River with the Zambezi saw twenty square kilometres of fertile flood plain vanish. The tell-tale signs are in the near-vertical river cliff. Since then, however, the floodgates have remained closed and the erosion and river widening have stopped.

Though it lies in unbearably hot tsetse-fly infested forest, riddled with a daunting array of tropical diseases including sleeping sickness, bilharzia, and malaria, many consider Mana Pools National Park, some seventy kilometres downstream from Chirundu, the jewel in Zimbabwe's crown.

Here the river, moving slowly north towards Zambia for thousands of years, has left behind the remains of old river channels forming small seasonal ponds and pools spread over an area of more than 2,000 square kilometres.

These reach back from the river for several kilometres where, on fertile terraces, huge mahogany and acacia trees cast luxuriant shade. Mana Pools is the stage for one of Africa's greatest natural spectacles — a classic theatre of the wild, attracting hordes of animals during the long, hot African summer, drawn by the abundance of water and the still lush grazing along its banks.

Above: Vervet monkey at Mana Pools.

Above: After travelling many kilometres from their drought-stricken hills, an elephant herd arrive at the shores of Lake Kariba.

One of Zimbabwe's two World Heritage Sites, the national park which lies between 1,300 feet and 3,000 feet above sea level is a timeless legacy of wilderness Zimbabwe that may yet be the last vestiges of a unique ecosystem.

A hydroelectric dam planned for Mapata Gorge will create an 850-square-kilometre lake, destroying most of the flood plain, and halve the carrying capacity of Mana Pools — the ecological heart of this great natural treasury.

There are other critical pressures. Poaching, especially of the Zambezi's unique fish populations as well as ivory and rhino horn, is still endemic despite the dedication of Zimbabwe's game wardens, rangers, and scouts: some have died in the war against poachers. Then elephants, like humans, destroy the environment and wreak great change in the forests and woodlands.

There is also a plan to eradicate tsetse-fly in the Mana Pools and Sapi wildlife areas to answer the continuing demand for land for human settlement. And oil prospecting companies have been given large tracts for exploration.

Opposite: Saucer, a familiar elephant at Chikwenya Safari Camp downstream from Mana Pools, pauses for lush pickings before inspecting the camp's dining area. During the dry season the elephant browse line is clearly visible forty-five feet above the ground.

Above: Burchell's zebra. Zebra stripes are as unique and individual as human fingerprints. None are alike.

All this poses an immense threat to the viability and survival of this marvellous, unique ecosystem. And reconciling the different interests may prove insurmountable. But few would count the cost of attempting to do so. Mana Pools deserves to survive unspoilt and unthreatened as it has for century after century.

Only open between April and October, the number of visitors is strictly controlled. There are no metal roads and only a few dirt roads. And apart from some limited accommodation at the park headquarters the only other place where you can stay is Chikwenya Camp, at the confluence of the Sapi with the Zambezi.

The sanctuary is home to more than 12,000 elephant — Zimbabwe's largest concentration after Hwange — 16,000 buffalo, and one of only two pockets of nyala in the country. Sadly, what was once Zimbabwe's finest population of black rhino has been virtually wiped out by poachers crossing the river from Zambia. For years, the desperate scenario here has been one of shoot to kill — the wardens, the poachers; the poachers, the wildlife.

Many other creatures flourish under its benign protection, however:

Above: Young elephant frolic in the waters of Lake Kariba not far from the shores of Bumi Hills.

thousands of zebra, kudu, impala, eland, and other antelope species among which the lion and the leopard, the hyena and wild dog find easy pickings.

Along the river bank, where one of the greatest varieties of birdlife in the world flourishes, sounders of hippo warm themselves in the morning sun. Later in the day, they keep cool by remaining all but submerged in the river, sharing their hidden sandbanks with silent and almost unseen crocodiles.

These great saurians, survivors from the age of the dinosaurs, are seen most often during the winter months between May and August when, because of the cold weather, they bask more frequently to raise their body temperatures to their preferred 30° Centigrade.

Croc families live in harems, with between eight and twelve females to one male. There are no sex chromosomes in crocodiles and to a great extent the temperature at which the eggs incubate governs the sex of the newborn. The ideal temperature for incubation is 31° Centigrade. The colder the nest, the more females the eggs produce. The warmer the nest, the more males.

Above: White-fronted bee eaters in the middle Zambezi Valley.

Formidable predators that move with amazing suddenness, a full grown crocodile can easily kill a full grown Cape buffalo. Tenacious of life, they do not die swiftly either. One crocodile's heart, cut out of the body, continued to beat for thirty minutes.

Distant mountains, the formidable escarpment wall of the valley, reed-edged backwaters and sandbanks flank the slow-moving Zambezi. The great number and variety of its woodland and water birds — more than 380 species — draws the breath of most ornithologists. Its banks are alive with Goliath herons, Egyptian and spurwing geese, cormorants, storks, brilliantly-coloured bee-eaters, and kingfishers.

Vultures, plovers, Nyasa lovebird, yellow-spotted nicator, white-collared pratincole, Livingstone's flycatcher, banded snake-eagle, and the clichéd symbol of Africa, the black and white fish eagle, haunt the riverine forest and mopane woodlands. In the river tigerfish, bream, tilapia, vundu, kupi, chessa, Cornish Jack, and lungfish sport and prey one upon the other.

The richness of the forest trees and plants is the vital link in Mana Pools chain of continuity. The apple ring acacia keeps the elephant herds alive during the fierce October-November dry season.

High up on the trees, almost forty-five feet above the ground, you can see the browse line where the elephants, standing on their rear legs, have raised their trunks to pluck the protein-rich pods. The seeds are recycled through the creature's dung to renew their pledge of plenty next year.

Most ubiquitous of all, however, is the odd-looking sausage tree with its pendulous fruit, weighing up to ten kilos (it gives quite a stunning headache when it falls on an unsuspecting head — as it often does). It has a great many uses that promote health. Applied to the flesh, its crushed and pulped fruit has been found to relieve skin cancer, and all over Africa it is an essential ingredient in herbal medicines concocted to treat a variety of ailments.

Baboon, rhino, and porcupine relish the fallen fruit and the beautiful, reddish-purple, trumpet-shaped flowers, pollinated by bats — almost one-third of Zimbabwe's 190 mammal species are bats — are a delicacy for many antelope and other creatures. Its wood is used to make the traditional dugout canoes of the local people.

Even in the broiling heat of early October days, at Chikwenya are something of an idyll. The safari camp run by longtime wilderness veteran Jeff Stutchbury and his wife is a masterpiece of simplicity. The basic mud-wall, lime plastered thatch huts are well spaced out on a terrace glade above the dry watercourse of the Sapi with shower and toilet open to the sky.

Giant elephant, given familiar names by Stutchbury and the staff, roam frequently through the camp investigating breakfast tables and guests, cookhouse and stores, providing memorable photo sessions for genial New York stockbrokers and Miami cabbies and their wives. Many of the females in the Mana Pools region do not have tusks and are much more aggressive than those with tusks.

As knowledgeable, and as eccentric, as Alan Elliott, Stutchbury keeps camp fires blazing throughout the season — from the cold frosty

Left: Elephant inspects cookhouse at Chikwenya Safari Camp downstream from Mana Pools National Park.

nights of the May-June-July winter to the 35° Centigrade evenings of late October and early November.

By the end of the season, the animals are so used to people and vehicles that they stand unmoving. But in the first weeks of April and May when the park re-opens after the six-month closure they are shy and easily disturbed.

'It's a bloody nuisance,' says one tour guide regular to Chikwenya. 'They just don't stand still long enough for our first clients to take pictures.' As she talks, Saucer, the almost resident male tusker, poses boldly, trunk raised above the breakfast table, for what seems to an inevitable morning photo session.

In the evening, Jeff calls guests from the dining table to the cookhouse to see their first honey badger, that fearsome, rarely seen, entrail ripper of African mythology, snout down in the waste water system. It has a beige-coloured cape stretching from snout to rump, now dirty from the delectable grease and filth it rummages through.

During a game drive in the forest, a sudden-seen leopard moves — in an all too brief flash of feline grace and sinew — from tree bole, through an open gully, into thick grass. Stutchbury leaves the open vehicle and stalks through the grass hoping to flush it out as the passengers, palpably excited Massachusetts housewives and jaded African writers, hold their breath and sit it out in almost unbearable tension.

Nobody notices the frenzied bites of the tsetse flies until next day when almost unbearably swollen ankles and arms are given the relief of

Above: Buffalo, perhaps the most ferocious of the Big Five when roused, in a Mana Pools swamp. The Cape buffalo has been responsible for the deaths of more hunters than any other species.

a dawn river cruise aboard the Stutchbury special: three fibreglass canoes joined together and bridged with a high deck to create a unique Zambezi sternwheeler.

Downstream he carefully slits a recently caught tigerfish, inserts some bottle corks, and then, imitating the haunting cry of the fish eagle, tosses the fish high into the air.

You watch where it falls and within seconds a fish eagle swoops down in one incredibly lithe movement to snatch it up with those terrible talons. The pictures will be fantastic and later Stutchbury drives to the base of the eagle's perch to recover the corks. Making guests happy is a special characteristic of all Zimbabwe's adventure safaris.

The boat drifts on down the broad sweep of the Zambezi, here five kilometres wide, swift-flowing currents raging beneath the deceptively-still surface. Chikwenya Island, all two square kilometres of it, is soon left behind as the boat veers into a reed and island strewn backwater on the northern side of the river where a profusion of stilts, plovers, egrets, the lily-trotting jacana, herons, and waders stalk water gardens of hyacinth and weed.

Opposite: Statue of the Tonga river god, Nyaminyami, whose wrath they say brought disaster to the construction crews who built the 420-foot-high, half a kilometre wide dam wall in the background below. The bodies of seventeen men swept away by a torrent of cement during epic floods in 1958 are entombed within the wall.

Above: Three man kapenta fishing rig heads for sea from Kariba town's Andora Harbour.

Masses of buffalo, elephant, impala, and other antelope haunt the thornbush and open glades of the banks against the smoky-grey Zambian mountains. During the season of the grass fires the air is misty with smoke and visibility limited.

As Stutchbury swings round an island peninsula a startled grazing hippo takes off at a canter and plunges ten feet into the water with a resounding, thunderous smack — a live, two-ton submersible in a startling high dive demonstration. Others raise their heads and yawn, revealing their frightening incisors. The yawn is not an intake of breath but an aggressive warning.

In this enchanted valley the season of drought is no more. Held back behind the wall of the Kariba dam, the Zambezi flows strong all the year round undercutting miniature cliffs of sand which occasionally crumble and avalanche into the water. Elsewhere, the honeycomb nests of the gregarious bee-eaters aerate the fragile cliffs, prelude to another cycle of erosion.

Their food chains secure and abundant, all life, including myriad butterflies, continues to prosper in this paradise where scores of

Left: Storm clouds over Lake Kariba, once the world's largest manmade lake. It covers more than 5,000 square kilometres of the middle Zambezi valley.

aquatic plants of overwhelming beauty — water primroses and yellow water peas among them — drift along many secret backwaters.

As you turn for home, the delicate pastel lavender of the morning glory water plant glows luminously in the weak and watery sun, yet another in an endless sequence of images that will never fade from the memory.

Few visitors, if any, drive to Chikwenya. The way in and out is by forty-five minute charter flight from Kariba and the air is turbulent as the Piper Aztec returning from Chikwenya climbs through the thermals over the rocky, arid Gotagota Hills to Kariba Airport.

It was at Kariba, no higher than 1,200 feet above sea level, that the Zambezi suddenly funnelled into the narrow neck of a 100-metre-wide gorge where it carved its way through a large granite block leaving the top to form a natural bridge.

The arch it formed gave the appearance of a large fish trap and the river people endowed it with the name 'Kariwa', the Shona word for the stone snare they use to catch birds and mice.

The first known written mention of the gorge is in a despatch of 11 December, 1667, from the Portuguese explorer Manuel Baretto. Almost 200 years after, on 20 October, 1860, David Livingstone and his brother shot the rapids, and almost exactly one century later, on 17 May, 1960, Britain's Queen Elizabeth, the Queen Mother, switched on Kariba's generators.

In a note to Lord Russell, Livingstone told of his hair raising three-hour ride. 'The wind rose and entered the gorge with great force, waves half filled my canoe and swamped Charley's but being near shore, nothing was lost.'

In 1877, after trekking along the Zambezi's north bank from Victoria Falls, Selous, the hunter, visited the gorge and William Keppel Stier, studying the possible route of a proposed railway along the Zambezi Valley that would link the river's navigable stretches, surveyed the gorge in 1892.

Nothing came of that idea but twenty years later, H. S. Kergwin, a government officer, suggested that it was an ideal place to dam the river for irrigation. The idea was eventually consigned to limbo only to be revived in 1941 when J. L. S. Jeffares made another survey, this time to determine the feasibility of a hydroelectric scheme.

Thirteen years later Richard Costain won the contract to build a town for 10,000 engineers and construction workers and Impresit, an Italian consortium, set about building the dam.

When the work began elders of the Tonga tribe who lived on the shores around the gorge petitioned the construction company to abandon the project. They said it would anger Nyaminyami, their river god, who would take revenge.

According to their tribal lore, Nyaminyami is the direct descendant of the Tonga soothsayers and witchdoctors who communicated telepathically and performed many miraculous cures. The Tonga believe that Nyaminyami is a benevolent spirit, the guardian of the river and all that it bestows life upon.

In 1958, when the river rose more than 100 feet and 3.5 million gallons a second raced through the gorge, washing away bridges and damaging the coffer dam, the elders claimed it was the vengeance of Nyaminyami.

On 20 February that year, when the floods were at the height, seventeen men — fourteen Africans and three Italians — were swept away by a wall of cement. Their bodies are still entombed within the tapering 420-foot-high dam wall which measures twenty-six metres thick at the base and thirteen metres wide at its crest.

At least another seventy people (the first an Italian, Pietro Giovanna, on 7 October, 1956, and the last, an African named simply Felikisi, on 15 December, 1961) died during the five years it took to complete the dam.

Dry season conditions were equally appalling. When temperatures reached more than 50° Centigrade workers had to keep their tools in buckets of water so that they could handle them.

Six flood gates are contained within the wall which stretches more than half a kilometre across the gorge and contains more than a million cubic metres of concrete and 11,000 tonnes of steel.

Lake Kariba itself was born on 3 December, 1958, when the diversion tunnel and temporary openings in the dam wall were closed but it was almost another five years, in September, 1963, before the lake attained its present dimensions.

It is 281 kilometres long and at its widest point more than forty kilometres across, making it for some years the largest manmade lake in the world. Covering more than 5,000 square kilometres, its jade-coloured waters, are studded with islands, and fringed by mountains and forests.

During the five years that it took to form it inspired Operation Noah, one of the most dramatic rescue stories in animal history. As the waters rose many animals were trapped on rapidly disappearing islands. But led by Robert Fothergill, game rangers keeping vigil during the flooding organized a mercy mission that captured the world's imagination.

At the end, the team had ferried 5,000 creatures to safety. The operation involved the capture of small and medium-size antelopes and smaller creatures like the endearing bushbaby, and literally steering larger game like fourty-four black rhino and many elephants to the game sanctuaries that line its southern shores.

Lake Kariba wrought astonishing economic as well as physical change. Before it was formed the Zambezi Valley was an overhot, infertile, almost physically uninhabitable region of no return. Now it has become a playground for water-sport enthusiasts, its shores and islands teeming with countless animals and birds.

Its waters support more than forty different species of fish, including a sardine species endemic to Lake Tanganyika and Lake Victoria which has formed the base of a major fishing industry. And the generators it drives are vital to the national growth.

The dusty, rowdy construction camp that came into being on the seven hills around the southern side of the Kariba gorge (and subsequently the shores of the lake) has become one of Africa's smartest holiday resorts.

But Kariba offers holidaymakers much more than just a sunny, idyllic resort atmosphere. There is the supreme beauty of its surrounding landscapes, magnificent watersports — including some of the most

Above: Retired American enjoys a tourist game cruise on the wide reaches of the Zambezi River downstream from Kariba dam.

Above: Hippo on a sandbank in the Zambezi. These aquatic mammals of the pig family, whose name derives from the Greek word for river horse, are capable of submerging for up to six minutes.

exciting fishing in the world, water skiing, sailing, and scuba diving — and a wildlife spectacle that has few, if any, equals. It also has many sophisticated hotels, casinos, and restaurants.

The most upmarket residential area is on the Heights, where the smart, former executive residences of the construction company straddle the peaks and slopes of the hills. The summit — at the end of a spectacular hairpin road — offers tremendous panoramas over the lake and the dam wall and downstream gorge. Baboons crowd the forests and frequently cross the road and during the seasons the hills are aflame with jacaranda and flamboyant blossoms.

On the summit, with its open air cinema and country club, close to the neat little shopping centre with its supermarket and evangelistic hotel, stands the Church of St Barbara, built to honour those who died building the dam. The unique design — the shape of a coffer dam — means there are no exterior walls, only archways that serve as entrances. Inside the names of those who died are inscribed on commemorative plaques.

From the other side of The Peak you look down on the dam wall and the dark river gorge far below. Soon you reach it. Three decades of polishing have almost erased the inscription on the brass plaque unveiled by Queen Elizabeth, the Queen Mother, but the sun beating off it reflects the gleaming pride of the achievement that she honoured. It is hard to comprehend. By comparison with the lake behind it, the elegantly curved wall of the dam seems far too slender to have been the catalyst for such a large inland sea.

When you stand on the roadway that crosses the dam to Zambia you feel it tremble from the power of the giant turbines buried deep inside the wall of the gorge. More than eighty feet below, weed collects in the barriers that sieve the 350-foot-deep waters.

Andora, around the cliff, on the south side of the gorge is Kariba's busiest harbour. Large houseboats, majestic yachts, and kapenta fishing rigs berth here and the Kariba car ferry, *Sealion*, discharges its passengers and cars at the end of its twenty-two hour voyage down the length of the lake. Freighters, ferries, and charter vessels keep the harbour frenetic with activity as smaller craft from the islands in the bay dart in and out on various errands.

In 1989 the cost of chartering one of these floating pleasure palaces with a maximum of twelve passengers was around $800 a week. Charter and commercial craft are governed by strict regulations. Indeed, after one vessel sank with loss of life more than sixty vessels were deregistered. Lake police in sleek launches maintain regular patrols.

From Andora marinas and hotel resorts stretch away along the coves and inlets of the lake shore, including the sublimely graceful architecture of the exotic Portuguese-style Caribbea Bay Hotel, managed by Zimbabwe Sun, the country's largest hotel group.

Elsewhere in this region, it is the harsh and brutal land that stamps its brand upon man. The lake has had profound effects on the communities which for centuries have made their home in the Zambezi Valley, particularly the Tonga people.

Resettled many kilometres inland, they had to face the sudden transition from a fishing culture to that of agriculturist on land as mean as any in the world.

On the sixty-kilometre journey inland from Bumi Hills, skirting the borders of Matusadona National Park, the stony, leached soil reflects the hammer-heavy heat remorselessly back, like blows from a smithy's forge.

The baked earth and tsetse-fly thicket is cruel and unrelenting, and the traditional round, mud and thatch homesteads sit amid fields of choking dust. It is a harsh existence yet people are cheerful and welcoming. They make the most of nothing — usually the gift of a smile and a rare and precious mug of water that they have had to carry perhaps eight or ten kilometres.

Although boreholes, dams, clinics, schools, administrative offices, and about 1,600 kilometres of roads were built to serve the new area in the Zimbabwe hinterland, the move was traumatic. Before the lake was formed their traditions and lifestyles had changed little in centuries.

The Two-Toed Tonga Tribe, so called because many of the men suffer from a congenital aberration that means they have only two toes, eke a

Above: Tonga woman grinding millet flour.

Above: Maize cobs drying at a Tonga homestead in the harsh, sunbaked hinterland of Lake Kariba.

harsh living from the arid, infertile soils, bordering the Matusadona National Park. But the Tonga are hungry for progress. Within a few years they established more than sixty schools.

Nonetheless, much of their lifestyle remains almost feudal. The *nganga*, witchdoctor, plays a major role. But no chauvinism affects the pipe-smoking women of the matrilineal Tonga whose children adopt the maternal totem and whose sons inherit from the maternal uncle.

Tonga women love adornment. They pierce their ears and insert thorns, which are subsequently replaced by sticks of steadily increasing size to enlarge the hole.

During their initiation ceremonies it was traditional to remove the six upper front teeth and although men now spurn this ceremony, Tonga women still follow the practice. As soon as the second teeth have settled, girls are taken by their mother to the tribal 'dentist' who uses two axes to remove the teeth — one levered between them, the other to hammer them out. Hot porridge is served to ease the pain.

Tonga women also pierce holes in both lips which they enlarge by placing wooden plugs in them. Another custom is for children around the age of ten to pierce holes in their noses — girls use a mimosa thorn, boys a porcupine quill.

The solid wooden doors of Tonga homesteads are inscribed with delicate carving. When someone dies they are buried close to the front door with all their personal possessions and the family then awaits the return, in a year or two, of the spirit. To encourage this goats and chickens are sacrificed. Beer is brewed and the mourners dance on the grave — not with joy but to compact the earth — accompanied by singing.

But the greatest transformation that Lake Kariba has wrought upon the Zambezi Valley are the new and distinct ecosystems it created. The harsh, broken country of the rugged escarpment hills, combined with infertile soils and poor rainfall, attract browsers.

Its lush shoreline vegetation, a mixture of aquatic and land grasses, supports a profusion of life. Extensive pastures of nutritious grass between the high and low water levels have led to dramatic increases in elephants, buffalo, rhino, and smaller animals.

The drowned forests of the permanent shallows with their mats of Kariba weed, *Salvinia molesta*, encourage a proliferation of insects which attract many birds — and allow hippo and crocodile to increase without inhibition. The numbers of Kariba's aquatic mammals and reptiles are unsurpassed anywhere in the world.

Out in the main lake the depths teem with huge shoals of bream and predatory tigerfish. Kapenta — tiny, protein-rich sardines endemic to Lake Tanganyika and Lake Victoria — which were introduced in the late 1960s yield around 12,000 tonnes a year. The species has also become a vital link in the food chain of the tigerfish.

Feeding deep down on Kariba's endemic plankton during the day, the kapenta schools move up to the surface at night lured by the lights — one above the surface, and one beneath — hanging from the curiously-shaped fishing rigs, basically a steel deck welded on to two enormous pontoons. Alarmed, the fish sound and swim straight down into the net. When enough fish are concentrated, the alarm is triggered by suddenly dousing the lights and the net quickly winched in.

Conditions for the three-man crews are harsh but the rewards are comparatively high. During the night, far away out on the lake, the darkness is alive with thousands of bobbing, twinkling lights.

Before Kariba was formed, 1,000 square kilometres of land were cleared of trees to aid future trawling operations. It was thought that they would be useless and could also damage this new artificially-created ecosystem. In fact, what no ecologist could have known was just how important the drowned trees would become.

Research by the national parks' Fisheries Research Institute at Kariba, which monitors fish populations, has shown that the flooded trees, which constitute an area twice as large as the bottom surface, play a major role in Lake Kariba's productivity, supporting dozens of invertebrate species and algae.

These are essential links in the food chain that sustains Kariba's impressively-high fish populations and also many water bird species. Lake birds include egrets, kingfishers, little bee-eater, black-collared barbet, fish eagle, and herons such as Goliath heron.

Above: Traditional Tonga pipe which is smoked by the womenfolk.

177

Above: Young Tonga girl.

Eventually, of course, the trees will disappear and Kariba will undergo another major change of character, but not for a long time yet. Although they have been weakened by woodborers at water level, and broken down by the lake's sometimes fierce and unpredictable storms, the trees rot remarkably slowly. The bark of some is still supple thirty years after they were immersed by waters 100 feet deep and they will remain intact for many more years.

Kariba undergoes constant change. Waves continue to pound away earth cliffs on some shores and islands but in other areas they throw up sandy beaches. And the fairly constant lake levels of the 1980s encouraged the spread of large and important trees — Natal mahogany, tamarind, and acacia, in particular — along its shores.

Though a freshwater lake, Kariba has the same volatile nature as the sea. Its unpredictable waters can be extremely dangerous. Often glassy calm, in minutes sudden storms spring up and gale force winds drive waves as high as fourteen feet before them. Waterspouts rising to 300 feet create another perilous hazard.

When the lake was first formed the swamped vegetation swiftly raised the water's nutrient levels, causing such a sudden and unpredicted increase in the growth of *salvinia* that it threatened to engulf the entire lake.

At one time the weed covered fifteen per cent of the surface. But fears of a major ecological disaster proved groundless. As the vegetation rotted away, the nutrient levels fell and the grotesque floating carpets of weed shrank. They now cover less than two per cent of the water.

In fact, what remains serves as a catalyst for the spread of the nutritious torpedo grass which provides valuable grazing for fish when submerged, and for ungulates when exposed. Taking root on the little salvinia islands floating on the surface, the grass soon spread around the lake — an ideal seedbed that helped it to establish itself in the shoreline between the low and high water mark.

Now, as the lake rises and falls, the exposed pastures sustain enormous numbers of herbivores. The new ecosystems have proved to be benign and protective. Indeed, the entire length of Kariba's southern shores is virtually an enormous wildlife sanctuary, interspersed by protected safari areas where licensed hunting is allowed.

The road from Makuti descends to the lake through the hills that form the Charara Safari Area. At night, the sign announcing that the visitor is now in a nature reserve and warning that it is dangerous to leave the car is immediately justified, two kilometres out of Makuti, by the tuskers browsing along the road verge.

Three kilometres later a pride of lion are enjoying the warmth of the tarmac. Grudgingly they stir themselves and lope lazily off into the underbrush. The flash of a leopard's eyes in a tree a little beyond this point leaves you in no doubt that you have entered the wilderness.

Twelve islands in the centre of the lake, the crests of a range of flooded hills whose wildlife was cut off from the mainland, together form the twenty-two square kilometres of Sibilobilo Safari Area where infrequent sport hunting is occasionally allowed. The islands boast

Overleaf: Waterbuck make their furtive way to the safe shadows of night as the sun's last rays bathe the shores of Lake Kariba in gold.

Left: Monitor lizard on the shores of Lake Kariba.

impressive populations of buffalo, impala, sable antelope, zebra, and greater kudu.

On the mainland south-west of these islands, in the lee of Chizarira National Park, on the 1,080 square kilometres set aside in 1963 to form the Chete Safari Area, licensed hunters stalk a wide spectrum of animals characteristic of the Zambezi Valley, including elephant, buffalo, leopard, black rhinoceros, eland, sable antelope, greater kudu, bushbuck, duiker, impala, wart hog, and baboon. Bird species include fish eagle and marabou stork.

Chete is also an important centre for wildlife studies carried out by the Nuffield Research Centre at the mouth of the Mwenda River.

In the hills above, the well-wooded, broken country of remote Chizarira National Park makes game viewing difficult. The park, which has a range of wildlife including elephant, black rhinoceros, lion, leopard, cheetah, and roan and tsesseby, is dominated in the north-east by 4,500-foot-high Mount Tundazi.

As an 'island' of rivers, perennial springs, and natural springs, the sanctuary, in fact, has extended the westerly reach of several bird species including the rarely-seen taita falcon (present in some gorges), crowned eagle, fish eagle, brown hooded kingfisher, red-billed wood hoopoe, golden-tailed woodpecker, and Meyer's parrot.

But few visit the remote park. Difficult to reach, and then only by four-wheel drive vehicle, it lies fifty kilometres south-east of Binga and you need written permission to enter. If you get this far, however, game walks along the edge of the escarpment and its stunning river gorges are extremely rewarding.

Hunting rights in the neighbouring Chirisa Safari Area, dominated by the valley of the Sengwa River, a large, but seasonal stream that drains northwards into Lake Kariba, are leased by a safari hunting company.

The wide variety of animals on hand, including almost 10,000 elephant, buffalo, impala, black rhinoceros, lion, leopard, cheetah, wild dog, warthog, bushpig, zebra, and various antelope species, makes it a hunter's paradise.

The Sengwa Institute of Wildlife Research, established in 1970, has developed sophisticated radio-tracking systems to monitor the

Above: Wildebeest are known as the 'Clown of the Plains' because of its strange look.

movements of large animals like elephant and rhino. Research studies of wart hog, elephant, impala, tsetse, bats, small mammals, lion, buffalo, and kudu have been undertaken.

It is Matusadona National Park, where elephant, buffalo, impala, kudu, and waterbuck roam its 1,370 square kilometres with seeming disdain of man, however, that is the real showpiece of this unparalleled wilderness. Perhaps because only one-third is open to the public — and then only a limited number — and it is virtually inaccessible by road.

Formed out of the gaunt plateaux, one step above the lake on the Zambezi Escarpment, and the undulating hillocks of the lake shore, its southern boundary is studded with many hidden bays, coves, inlets, and backwaters. The Ume River forms the western boundary, and the flooded Sanyati gorge, carved by the Mutare river, the eastern boundary. Waterfalls plunge almost soundlessly 2,000 feet down the gorge's granite cliffs and only the haunting cry of the fish eagle and the bark of the baboon break the silence.

Matusadona is home to at least 400 black rhino, more than a

Opposite: Young elephant in mock combat at Bumi Hills. Zimbabwe is one of the last great strongholds of the elephant with an estimated 15,000 in Hwange National Park and around 12,000 in the Mana Pools National Park.

Above: Buffalo graze the luscious torpedo grass pastures on Lake Kariba's shores beneath Bumi Hills Safari Lodge.

Opposite: Buffalo herd in the marshlands of the Zambezi River. Egrets live in symbiosis with buffaloes and pachyderms like rhino and elephant, feeding off ticks and other parasites.

thousand elephant, several thousand buffalo, sable and roan antelope, greater kudu, bushbuck, eland, waterbuck, hippopotamus, lion, leopard, impala, hyena, and many crocodile. Its birds include fish eagle, African darter, cormorant, heron, stork, plover, lily trotter, and many woodland species.

Its shores border the largest mass of water on the lake and the most developed, Kariba's eastern basin. For fishermen many rivers offer fine sport and for both angler and holidaymaker there is the magnetic lure of many islands and the Sanyati Gorge.

There are no lodges or hotels in the park but many on its periphery. You travel either by boat or twenty-minute charter flight. Either way, you will get to know something of the character of the lake. From a height of 500 feet you look down on one island after another, small and large, some simply sand and scrub where the waterlines are clearly marked. Extensive forests of drowned trees — their bare limbs like something out of a Greek tragedy — stand in the shallows that stretch away from the shores.

The plane flies over the resort islands of Spurwing and Fothergill

Opposite: Cheetah are the fastest land animals in the world with recorded speeds of up to 112 kilometres an hour. They catch their prey with a slashing rake of the claws to the hind quarters.

Above: Leopard, the most secretive and stealthy of the large cats, usually hunt by night and lie up hidden during the day.

Overleaf: Lion cub. They are the only species of big felines to live in social groups. Lionesses tend to hunt and kill more often the males.

and the Tiger Bay fishing camp on the Ume River. At Spurwing's tented camp you wake to memorable vistas of the Matusadona Mountains and Sanyati Gorge across the water.

The experience is much the same at Fothergill — which also operates Chikwenya camp — except that guests sleep in African-style thatched chalets and at the end of 1989 it was not so much an island but once again an extension of the mainland to which it used to belong.

Tiger Bay fishing camp is all about what it says. The ultimate prize is the ferocious and lively tigerfish — the best specimens are found in Sanyati Gorge, venue of an annual international tigerfishing tournament.

By contrast, from the minute its rocky landing strip, lying between two granite hills, hoves into view you are left in no doubt that Bumi Hills Safari Lodge, just outside the park on the hills above the south-western banks of the Ume River, is all about wildlife.

Usually there's an impressive collection of elephant or buffalo, and other animals, which have to be chased away by lodge staff before

*Above: Darter on tree at Lake Kariba's Water
Wilderness.*

you land. Even though guests accustomed to more routine landing
approaches may find the experience unnerving, those in search of
wildlife should need no more convincing that they have come to the
right place.

Those with any doubts remaining, however, only have to take a
game drive with one of the lodge's resident rangers. Five minutes is
all you need. Elephant come close enough to your open vehicle for
you to lay your hand upon them — if you are brave or unwise
enough.

Greater kudu, with perhaps the most magnificent horns in the
animal kingdom, majestic lyrate proclamations of their male
chauvinism, stand motionless in the thicket. Wart hog, tails erect, trot
briskly away and buffalo cover the grassy river banks and the forest
thickets in their thousands.

At sundown, Daniel, a Zimbabwean ecologist, parks the vehicle and
offers beers or soft drinks as the sky is burnished red beyond a herd of
200 buffalo at the water's edge.

Next day you drift on the gentle Kariba swell in a power boat no

Above: Hippo skull.

more than three metres from two young bull elephants who for the last three hours have been frolicking in mock combat, in deep water a kilometre offshore.

Ivory clacking and clicking as they wrestle, the two frequently submerge, before bobbing up. Nowhere else in the world can you watch this behaviour at such close quarters.

Older animals of the herd migrate regularly between the mainland and the islands, some preferring a solitary life there as lotus eaters on their own desert strip to the vagaries of mainstream 'city' life.

When elephants swim they move slowly in a running movement, the herd in single file, touching up against the rumps, or holding the tails of those in front. Underwater, they have an uncanny sense of direction.

It has been recorded that two elephants once travelled forty kilometres across the lake, from Zimbabwe to Zambia, virtually submerged all the way with their trunk serving as a snorkel, on a swim that lasted twenty-three hours.

As you make your way back to your room later that evening, after nightcaps in the lodge's garden bar, the shadowy tree standing by the garden path turns out to be a full grown tusker. The golden rule says, 'don't move'. Overruling instinct sends you sprinting down the nearest staircase. At Bumi Hills man remains ever the intruder.

The lodge is also the base for perhaps the most unforgettable experience of any *Journey through Zimbabwe* — tranquil nights under the stars at Water Wilderness.

In the morning, however, the sound of crashing breakers and a tormented wind straining at the casement wakes you. White caps are visible far out on the lake below.

Out of the harbour, the fibreglass boat pitches and tosses as it corkscrews through a wild sea beneath racing clouds. Bow thrusting into the breakers under half power, the vessel sails way out into the lake before the helmsman judges the pitch of the waves and adroitly turns beam on to race for the shelter of the Matusadona shoreline.

Soon the sea slackens and the boat creams between drowned trees and marker buoys to the Water Wilderness 'mother ship' moored in a deep lagoon. Around it, tethered to the stumps of drowned trees, each floating on its own steel pontoons, are four comfortable self-contained rooms.

Days at Water Wilderness are like a Robinson Crusoe idyll. You paddle your own canoe — to your room and back for meals, and on game voyages. Twenty-three-year-old Spike Williamson, a protege of Allan Elliott and Jeff Stutchbury, son of a late ecologist who specialized in the study of elephants, is the resident manager, guide, and host. Far from the madding crowd, Spike revels in his remote and isolated animal kingdom.

Drifting in the Water Wilderness launch he unfolds his encyclopaedic knowledge of Zimbabwe's nature — its trees, insects, beasts, and birds. Standing two metres away in the shallows five bull elephants pluck out clumps of torpedo grass and clear away the mud from the roots with a rhythmic swish-swish of their trunks.

Over a home cooked dinner that evening — the drinks are on the

Opposite: Twin mirror-reflections glowing on Lake Kariba's waters as the sun sinks beneath the far horizon.

house — eaten by the flickering light of a hurricane lamp, Spike's profound love and knowledge of wild Africa murmurs quietly on the still air to the lullaby of chirping cicada, croaking frogs, and the plop of fish breaking water.

In the hours of tranquillity at Water Wilderness there are always adrenalin-charged experiences — be it the snout of a crocodile nosing by your canoe at night or the sudden emergence of a hippo coming up for air as you drift through a moonspun silver thread on the still water of the lagoon.

Next morning at dawn you follow Spike Indian file in your fibreglass canoe and beach it on the shore of a hidden backwater for another session of tranquillity and adrenalin in equal measure.

Gun in hand he leads his party inland over a rise through scrub and stunted woodland, pausing to point out the spoor of a recent leopard, the tunnel trap of the driver ant, and skirt two lone but ferocious buffalo.

Though they are more than 100 metres distant, the New York financier and his wife choose to head for a hide perched in a tree to await Spike's return. The bark of the baboon pack startles them. The leopard is still around. And the adrenalin pumps through their veins like a Zambezi flood.

Late that afternoon, the sun burns its haunting vermilion insignia into Water Wilderness — a flaming arrow that sears the forest of drowned trees and turns the water a molten crimson. Never were you more alone — and never were you closer to the world as it perhaps once was and should always be. And the words of Robert Browning echo through the mind:

> *Just when we are safest, there's a sunset touch*
> *A fancy from a flower-bell, someone's death,*
> *A chorus ending from Euripedes, —*
> *And that's enough for fifty hopes and fears*
> *As old and new at once as nature's self*
> *To rap and knock and enter in our soul*